COCKTAILS
& PERFECT
PARTY
DRINKS
SUSY ATKINS

Quadrille

A word on measures

Each cocktail recipe makes up a large drink for one. Simply multiply by the number of guests. I have not stipulated the amount of wine for each and every occasion, but as a general rule of thumb err on the generous side, providing half a bottle of wine each for parties with food and one bottle each for wild, boozy nights. It's very bad news to run out. Buy 'sale or return' and you can't go wrong!

First published in 2005 by
Quadrille Publishing Ltd
Alhambra House
27–31 Charing Cross Road
London WC2H 0LS

Editorial Director Jane O'Shea
Creative Director Helen Lewis
Project Editor Lisa Pendreigh
Designer Claire Peters
Illustrator Evelina Frescura
Production Controller Ruth Deary

Cataloguing in Publication Data: a catalogue record for this book
is available from the British Library.

ISBN 1 84400 222 5

Printed in China

CONTENTS

Introduction **8**

1 The Classic Cocktail Party **10**

2 The Dinner Party **26**

3 Summer Picnics & Al Fresco Parties **44**

4 Christmas, New Year & Thanksgiving Parties **60**

5 Girls' & Boys' Parties **80**

6 Weddings, Christenings & Birthday Parties **92**

7 The Big Boozy Bash **110**

8 Out On The Town **126**

9 The Morning After… **142**

Party Snacks **156**   Best Brands **158**

Index **159**   Acknowledgements **160**

INTRODUCTION

As a drinks writer, I am often asked for advice by my friends. Actually, they rarely ask for help in choosing the right wine for a quiet night in – I guess they know what they like when they crack open a bottle with supper or in front of the TV – but I *am* regularly called in when they are planning a party.

Suddenly, drinks seem very important: what styles to choose, where to get them, how to store and serve them. 'Help!' they all cry, whether they're getting married, having an anniversary bash, organising the annual office night out, or celebrating a big birthday. This is the social ritual of drinking together (whether calmly or wildly) and clearly it's worth worrying over.

Quite right, too. There's no point sending out beautiful invitations, cooking fabulous food or hiring the best DJ in the world, only to serve horrible drinks! Pull off the perfect drinks, though, and your party will go with much more of a swing. This means understanding the basics about wine, spirits and cocktails, learning how certain drinks suit certain occasions and why some styles are seasonal. It means matching wines to food and it even means matching drinks to your guests!

Sometimes the world of drinks, especially wine, can seem intimidating. This book isn't like that. It doesn't plan to turn you into a wine snob, just to give you some easy, accessible facts about wine styles and the basics on how to make cocktails. There's lots on how to get value for money from party drinks, along with tips on being a dazzling host. There's even a chapter on the best way to tackle a big night on the town, including how to navigate a wine list (essential reading for anyone who has the scary job of ordering for a crowd).

Wherever possible I've avoided obscure or expensive drinks. The cocktails are not too complex; the wines are not too rare or venerable. There is plenty here that's exciting, exotic and enticing to drink, without including bottles that no one can afford or even find in the shops. The idea is to gain access to drinks that work well at parties – and parties should be about everyone relaxing and having fun, including the host. Enjoy this book, and enjoy your party.

1 the classic cocktail party

In case you've been living on Mars for the past few years,
cocktails are back in vogue!
Cities teem with new, funky cocktail bars
manned by young, trendy 'mixologists'
stirring and shaking the latest concoctions.
You can make them, too.
Start with the timeless great recipes, still revered by all.
Here they are – the classic cocktails.

THE LOWDOWN

You'll never understand much about cocktails until you've tackled the classics.
Why? Because they give you a firm base of knowledge to build upon. Learn the most popular traditional recipes, throw in a few modern classics, and you are halfway to mastering the whole topic. You'll know which fruits go best with which spirits, which glasses suit which style of drink, and when to shake or stir. Some of the basic rules of the recipes that follow can be adapted again and again as you start playing around and creating your own clever concoctions to suit your parties.

I could have chosen from hundreds of well-loved cocktails. But for parties, some work better than others – avoid those that mean buying very expensive or obscure ingredients in large volume, those that taste too far-out and bizarre, and those that are too complex to make when hosting a crowd. Instead, kick off by discovering the ultimate crowd-pleasers to wow all your guests, the ones that look good, either because they're colourful or fizzy (for extra razzamatazz), and the recipes which cover a wide range of spirits (so you're a versatile host).

The idea is to balance sweet with sour (bitters, fruit acids) and still let the taste of a good spirit come through. So here are eight all-time greats to kick things off. There are more cocktail recipes throughout this book, but especially in chapters 3 (summery cocktails); 4 (winter ones); and 5 (frivolous girlie ones). Get shakin'…

 THE **Kit** If you've never made cocktails before, you will need to stock up a bit here – but just a bit. First, buy yourself a **metal cocktail shaker** with a tight-fitting lid. Okay, you can use a big clean jam-jar if you want, but it won't look sophisticated! Ideally, you will have a **glass stirrer** or long spoon for, well, stirring, and a special instrument for 'muddling' – mushing up ingredients like fruit or mint leaves. A **pestle** or the end of a small rolling pin will do fine for the latter. Have a small **sharp knife** handy for cutting and paring fruit, and prepare **ice cubes** with bottled water, not tap, which can taste of chemicals. Keep **sugar** and sugar cubes at the ready.

For the record, the most famous conical cocktail glass is the **martini glass**, a slender **flute** is used for Champagne cocktails and a **highball**, or tall, straight-sided tumbler, is for longer drinks, like Gin Fizz. That said, anything goes in your own home. Chill glasses by storing them in the fridge or loading them with crushed ice for a few minutes before chucking the ice away.

Don't worry too much about investing in lots of different, pricey ingredients straightaway. To start, you will need just one or two **spirits**, maybe a small bottle of **bitters** (which will last a long time) and one piece of **fruit**. You can even make some **sugar syrup** (see page 25). Build up a collection of posh ingredients slowly. Pick quality spirits (see page 158) and the freshest fruits.

Appearance counts, so make lovely **garnishes** using fruit zest, berries, olives and so on. Dip the moistened rims of glasses into saucers of salt or fine sugar as you wish, or pare the peel of fruit to give wonderful twirls of zest.

CHAMPAGNE COCKTAIL

1 **sugar cube**
dash of **Angostura bitters**
10ml **good quality brandy**
125ml **chilled Champagne**

Place the sugar cube at the bottom of a tall, slender Champagne flute and dash with the Angostura bitters. Pour in the brandy and top up with Champagne. Serve immediately while the bubbles are lively.

TIP **Use dry cava or other decent sparkling wine instead of Champagne – it will taste nearly as good and cost much less. But make sure it is dry – 'brut' on a label indicates this.**

PERFECT FOR   Sophisticated, luxurious small parties

COSMOPOLITAN

50ml **plain or citrus vodka**

30ml **Cointreau**

15ml **lime juice**

10ml **cranberry juice**

Place all the ingredients in a cocktail shaker with several ice cubes.
Stir gently and strain into a chilled cocktail glass.

TIP **Garnish with a twist of fresh lime or orange peel – try to carve the peel so it curls beautifully!**

PERFECT FOR   Kicking off a classy cocktail evening

DAIQUIRI

40ml **white rum**
juice of 1 **lime**
sugar or **sugar syrup** to taste

Shake the ingredients over ice and strain into a chilled cocktail glass.

TIP **Try a fruitier, colder version. For the classic Frozen Strawberry Daiquiri, add extra sugar syrup and four or five strawberries to the above ingredients. Blend with a handful of ice then strain into your cocktail glass.**

PERFECT
FOR
Summer evening parties on the lawn

GIN FIZZ

30ml **lemon juice**
10ml **sugar syrup**
1 tsp **sugar**
50ml **gin**
soda water

Shake up the lemon juice, sugar syrup, sugar and gin in a cocktail shaker. Strain into a tall highball glass half-filled with ice cubes then top right up with soda water.

TIP **For extra body and silkiness, add 20ml lightly whipped egg white, shaking it with the other ingredients. Or make the basic recipe with whisky rather than gin, perhaps using lemonade instead of soda.**

PERFECT FOR Lazy, slightly sozzled Sunday house parties

MANHATTAN

40ml **American rye whiskey**
20ml **sweet vermouth**
2 dashes **Angostura bitters**
1 **maraschino cherry**

Stir the whiskey, vermouth and bitters over ice in a jug or a cocktail shaker. Strain into a chilled martini glass and garnish with the maraschino cherry.

TIP **For a dry Manhattan, use dry vermouth and garnish with lemon peel. For a 'southern' flavour, use smokey, sweet bourbon whiskey. Make it with brandy instead, and you have a Harvard!**

PERFECT FOR Cold evenings in with your best friends

MARGARITA

40ml **tequila**
25ml **Cointreau**
25ml **fresh lime juice**

Shake the ingredients together over ice and strain into salt-rimmed glasses. To make salt-rimmed glasses: pour plenty of coarse grained salt into a saucer, rub a slice of fresh lime on the outside rim of the glass, and dip the rim into the salt.

TIP **For a Frozen Margarita, put everything in a blender with some crushed ice and blitz together.**

PERFECT FOR Frivolous drinking and dancing with your best mates

MARTINI

1 large dash **French dry vermouth**
50ml **gin**
1 **stoned olive** (in brine)
or **thin lemon peel** to garnish

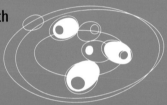

Pour the vermouth and gin into a cocktail shaker with lots of ice cubes.
Stir well for a good minute. Strain into a chilled martini glass and garnish.

TIP **No other cocktail is as controversial (or personal) as the Martini.
This is an extra-dry gin version that I like. Work out your perfect
recipe, perhaps with extra vermouth, a dash of bitters or a teaspoon
of sugar syrup. Or shaken… not stirred!**

**PERFECT
FOR** Breaking the ice, quickly

TEQUILA SUNRISE

half a **fresh lime**
50ml **tequila**
100ml **chilled smooth orange juice**
2 dashes **grenadine**

Squeeze the lime over ice cubes in a large highball glass. Add the
tequila and orange juice. Finally pour in the rosy grenadine very gently,
so it remains somewhat separate.

TIP **Try making a Sunrise the old-fashioned way, using fresh lemon
juice instead of orange (you may want to add a little sugar syrup,
too) or with crème de cassis instead of grenadine.**

PERFECT Birthdays and other happy celebrations
FOR

THE PERFECT HOST
TIPS

Q HOW FAR IN ADVANCE CAN I MAKE COCKTAILS?

A As close as possible to the moment they are sipped – while they are 'still laughing' as someone once put it, poetically. Have everything possible ready in advance and create them then and there, in front of your guests. It makes a great show…

Q SHAKE OR STIR?

A Good question – and one that has been asked by every generation. Shaking the ingredients in a shaker half-filled with ice chills the drink down rapidly and slightly dilutes it. Shake for between 5 and 10 seconds only. Strain into a glass. Stirring (in the shaker, usually, and for one minute or longer) dilutes the drink more. Some experts say that frivolous, light, slightly frothy cocktails like Daiquiris and Margaritas should be shaken, as this aerates them lightly, while more serious, silky-smooth ones like Martinis should be stirred, coolly. But as always, it's up to you.

 WHERE CAN I FIND SUGAR SYRUP?

A Buy sugar syrup ready made in bottles, or make your own. Fill a clean cocktail shaker with 50/50 fine caster sugar and water. Close and shake for one minute to dissolve most of the sugar. Leave to stand for 5 minutes, then shake again and use, or store in the fridge for up to one month.

DO I NEED TO BOTHER WITH ALL THOSE GARNISHES, ICE CUBES, CHILLED GLASSES AND SO ON?

A Yes, yes, yes – and even more so for parties rather than solitary drinking. Think of it as a performance, with these as your props. And take care to use good quality (preferably organic, unwaxed) fruit and herbs for garnishes, bottled water, not tap, for ice, and try coarse sea salt for glass rims.

2 THE DINNER PARTY

If you are planning to show off some serious cooking to friends and family, it's important to pick the best bottles. Matching food and drink is an art; the correct pairing can enhance the flavours of both. Don't be intimidated by it though – it's easy to get right. Here's how to pick the perfect drinks for a wonderful dinner party.

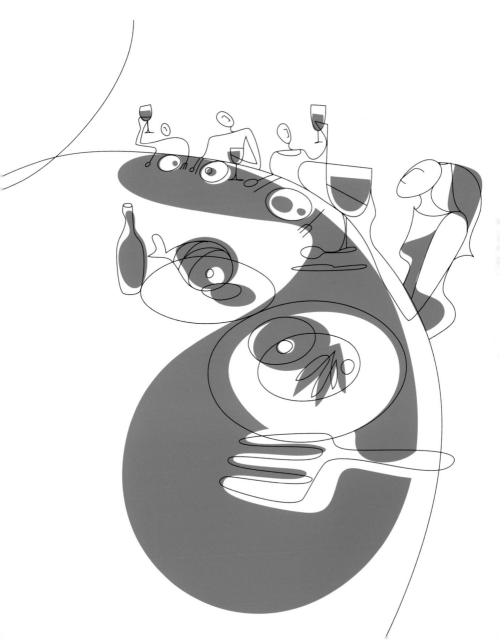

28

This chapter is all about the great sociable ritual of dining together. The drinks can be just as important as the food, although that tends to be forgotten as hosts immerse themselves in yet another celebrity chef's cookbook. But think about it; your food can only be enhanced by the right choice of drink.

It's just not just about matching food and wine at the table. Refreshing, mouthwatering aperitifs should set you up for the feast ahead. And after-dinner drinks deserve some thought too, as this is the chance to open something original and special to wind down over. Neither aperitifs nor after-dinner drinks need to be old-fashioned – here you'll find plenty of inspiring, modern ideas for both.

In between are the drinks – mainly wines – to wash down your feast. Forget hard and fast rules about food and wine matching! Plenty of bottles match many dishes. But some work better than others and a few simple guidelines help to tease these great partnerships out. The aim is to marry your food and wine well, to bring natural pairs together rather than have them worlds apart in flavour, style and balance. Get it right and the food and wine will become more than the sum of their parts.

THE LOWDOWN

THE Kit

The right dinner glasses certainly add to our enjoyment of drink, otherwise we might as well use plastic tumblers. So what makes a 'good' wine glass? Ideally, it is **plain crystal**, not cut, so you can view the wine. **Clear glass**, not coloured, is a sensible choice for the same reason. And choose **thin glass**, rather than chunky, thick glass, as this looks better and feels nicer on the lips.

Choose wine glasses with **tall stems**. If you then hold a glass by its stem (as wine experts do), you can swirl the liquid a little, like a pro, releasing its aromas. That way, you won't warm up the wine with your sticky hands! Don't fill up wine glasses more than one-third, so you can swirl easily. **Tall glasses** look more elegant, too.

It pays to have **more than one glass** per person. That said, no one wants to spend all day washing and polishing fifty different wine glasses. Two per person should be fine – one **smaller glass** for aperitifs *and* white wine at dinner (carry the glass to the table) and one **larger glass** for red. Provide **tall flutes** for sparkling wine if you want to, but the smaller white wine glass will be perfectly okay if you don't. You can even wash the same white wine glass for dessert wines, port or liqueurs later on. Avoid tiny stingy schooners for liqueurs – very out-of-date!

Don't forget the rest of your kit! Have a good **corkscrew** handy, and a **decanter** if you are using one (see page 65). If you have any fancy wine accessories to show off, such as a **bottle coaster**, this is the perfect occasion to bring them out and make the table look fine.

aperitifs

The drink your guests quaff before eating must get their juices flowing. Choose drinks with a tangy quality – a crisp streak of acidity – for that **mouthwatering, palate-cleansing** edge. Chilling the wine brings out this succulence.

Bubbles only enhance the refreshing appeal of a wine (it's the lively way the fizz froths in the mouth) so **sparkling wine** is a great idea early on. Serve a renowned label from **Champagne** if you're splashing out, or try zesty **cava** from Spain for good value. Dry wines taste fresher and cleaner than sweet ones, so pick a fizz that says '**brut**' on the label. You'll find loads more tips on sparkling wine in Chapter 6.

Alternatively, serve **still white wine**, which has the advantage that you can carry it through to go with the starter at dinner. The best styles here are **light, unoaked, dry and crisp**. Avoid oaky Chardonnay at this stage – too heavy. **Dry Riesling, Sauvignon Blanc, premium Muscadet** and **light Italian whites** are all clever choices.

Other star aperitifs

• **Fino or manzanilla sherry** – the driest, palest styles of all fortified wines. Tangy and brisk, a great pick-me-up. Serve with salty snacks.

• **Cold beer** – pick premium quality lager, perhaps Czech, or a more 'hoppy' English ale for a slightly bitter twist.

• **Gin and tonic** – the classic long aperitif, simple, dry and mouthwatering. Add loads of fresh lemon slices and ice.

• **Dry gin-based cocktails** – those that are simple and fresh-tasting, like Martinis, work best prior to eating.

• **Soft aperitifs** – should have that tangy, clean, dry character, too. Try cranberry juice or elderflower pressé.

• **Dry Madeira** – choose a style called Sercial, served chilled.

• **White port** – mix with tonic and loads of ice. Serve with salted almonds.

• **Very sweet pudding wine** – surprisingly, a dessert wine like Muscat de Beaumes de Venise, served very cold in small quantities, can be a great choice before dining.

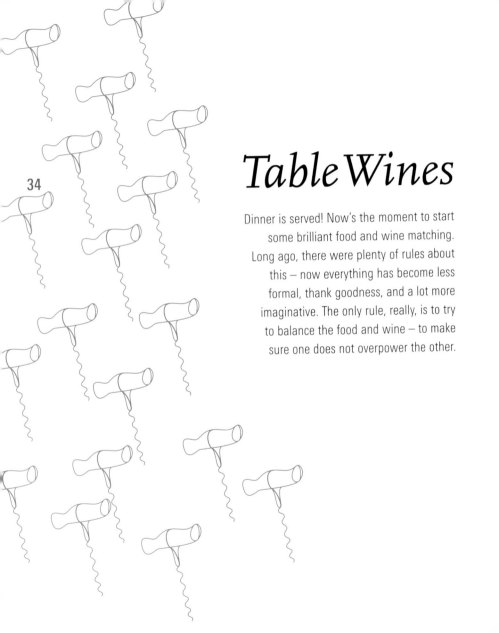

Table Wines

Dinner is served! Now's the moment to start some brilliant food and wine matching. Long ago, there were plenty of rules about this – now everything has become less formal, thank goodness, and a lot more imaginative. The only rule, really, is to try to balance the food and wine – to make sure one does not overpower the other.

If your starter is light and delicate – a simple, fresh prawn dish, say – crack open a **light, easy-going white wine**. If, however, you are serving rich meaty antipasto or aromatic smoked salmon with Irish soda bread, you'll need a **medium red wine** or a **full-bodied, oaky white wine**.

Ditto, the main course – don't think just about the main ingredient, but **consider the whole dish**. Chicken breasts with lemon sauce demand an **easy-drinking, fruity white**, while chicken in a rich red wine, garlic and smokey bacon sauce goes much better with a **fairly powerful aromatic red**.

Be canny and try to **consider the wine when you are planning the menu**, rather than thinking about it ten minutes before dinner starts. Too often, tables groan with different bottles and guests end up helping themselves to wines that don't show off the food at all. So be organised: plan a starter that works well with the **aperitif wine**, so that guests can bring their glasses through to the table and you can carry on pouring from the same bottle. Then make a very definite **switch to red** – and different glasses – for the main course. Without being too bossy, **steer your guests** towards the wines you have chosen.

With cheese or pudding, keep it simple. If you're serving a cheese course, it makes sense to **stick to one red** throughout – one that suits the main course and the cheese and biscuits. Or open a **port** after the table reds have been enjoyed. For **pudding wine**, you'll need to provide clean glasses or make sure everyone swills out red wine dregs with water. Again, good balance is essential:

• Don't serve a cloying, heavy sweet wine with a light, fresh fruit salad. Choose something more **delicate**, such as a **sweet Riesling** from a cool climate.

• Pick **rich dessert wines**, such as fortified **Muscats** or **sweet sherries**, to go with hearty baked puddings.

• The most prized and **complex honeyed wines**, like **Sauternes** and **Tokaji**, deserve simple but top-notch desserts to show them off. Pair with homemade chocolate-, coffee- and nut-flavoured puddings, or Italian treats like panettone.

• Serve very **light sparklers**, such as **Asti**, with a delicate fresh dessert for some light relief if the whole meal has been rich and heavy.

• Consider serving just a **fine pudding wine** *in place of* dessert. Quite often you simply don't need another course. Make a fuss of a special sweet wine, opening it at the table, and you won't want more food.

THE DINNER PARTY

Different but delicious

Of course, you don't have to drink wine with dinner. Why not be original and widen the choice? Here are some exciting ideas:

• Instead of wine, try **premium farmhouse cider** with **pork casseroles** and **baked hams** for a lovely ripe appley quality to the drinks. This works especially well when the pork or ham is in a fruity sauce or comes with a fruity chutney.

• **Cider** and **beer** are excellent matches for **cold cuts of meat** and **salad** with all the trimmings. Drink **good ale**, especially if you're dining on meat cooked in it – for example, beef in beer casserole.

• There are loads of great **wines** that go with **spicy Indian** and **Thai** food. Try Gewürztraminer, Sauvignon Blanc and lighter, fruity Chardonnays for whites, or **soft, ripe Aussie reds**. But you could also crack open **white (wheat) beer**, as its soft yeasty character complements spicy food. Or stick to **premium lager**, especially with very hot dishes.

• **Chinese** food teams nicely with **off-dry white wines**, but do try **apple juice, ginger drinks** or **lime cordial** instead, all of which go remarkably well.

• Never pass up the chance to serve a drink of the same origin as your cuisine – for example, **sake** goes wonderfully well with **Japanese food**, **Mexican beer** with **Tex-Mex**, and **Belgian beer** with **moules frites**. They grew up side-by-side and have evolved into great dinner party companions, so try to stick to them!

Don't forget to have **water** on hand at all times (you can provide separate tumblers, but it's not compulsory). Still or sparkling in glass bottles is best, although you can tart up half-decent tap water with slices of lemon and lime and ice. Always provide soft drinks as an option – a jug of **ginger ale**, **homemade lemonade** or **elderflower cordial** are alternatives to highly acidic orange juice. Avoid soft drinks with very strong flavours, as they can overpower your cooking. Cola with lemon sole, anyone? Didn't think so...

Size matters

Finally, when planning wines for dinner, do consider serving **larger bottles**. A **magnum** (two 75cl bottles; in other words, 1.5 litres) looks impressive and generous, and can be a talking point. It should cost no more than two normal bottles. Try an even bigger size if you dare – a **jeroboam** is 3 litres, for example. A dinner party is the perfect time to think big.

AFTER DINNER DRINKS

Of course, you can simply carry on drinking table wines after dinner, but it's much more appealing (and impressive) to offer guests something quite different at this point. Here you want the opposite of an aperitif – the aim is not to quench the thirst or get the mouth watering, but to provide intriguing and lingering flavours to savour.

After-dinner drinks need plenty of flavour to shine through after a big feast. Usually guests don't want large quantities to drink at this point, so crack open something **concentrated** and **flavour-packed** – a drink just right for sipping in small glasses.

For all these reasons, **richly fortified wines** are ideal. Choose a **red port** (ruby is the cheapest, but try to upgrade to LBV – late-bottled vintage – or vintage styles for better quality), a **tawny port** (aged in oak for a mellow, nutty character), a **rich sherry** (try sweet or dry oloroso) or **malmsey Madeira** (the sweetest Madeira). Otherwise, consider a **fine single malt** (choose something with bags of smoky character, from Islay perhaps), a **premium French brandy**, either **Cognac** or **Armagnac**, or **Calvados**, made from apples. **Brandy** from Jerez in Spain is rich, sweet and generally good quality, too.

Sweet cream liqueurs can be seriously cloying after a big meal and are increasingly naff, so offer a more **grown-up liqueur** – **Benedictine** and **Chartreuse** are both wonderfully complex and herbal, **Cointreau** and **Grand Marnier** have warming citrus flavours, while **Amaretto** is deliciously nutty. **Bourbon whiskey** from Kentucky would be deeply cool, of course: its charred, honeyed-vanilla flavour means it appeals to those with a slightly sweet tooth. For more on after-dinner drinks, turn to pages 76–7.

THE PERFECT HOST
TIPS

Q WHAT SHOULD I DO IF GUESTS BRING THEIR OWN (HORRIBLE) BOTTLES OF WINE TO HAVE WITH DINNER?

A Tell them not to in advance! Shamelessly demand flowers or chocolate instead, but if they insist, ask them to bring a specific style. Suggest they bring a Sancerre or a sparkler, say, as an aperitif. If they still bring something naff, put it to one side and conveniently forget about it. Or – in a desperate moment – drop it!

Q I'M READY TO SERVE A NEW, DIFFERENT WINE AT THE TABLE BUT SEVERAL PEOPLE HAVEN'T FINISHED UP THE LAST ONE, SO CAN I SIMPLY MIX THEM?

A No! Both wines will taste completely different – and wrong – if they are mixed. Invite your guests to drink up or fetch new glasses. If you are having a serious wine-tasting session over dinner, it's perfect manners to provide a jug for leftovers. Indeed, if guests are driving, or simply want to try several wines without drinking too much, it's a great idea to dump any dregs and move on.

Q I'M SERVING SPARKLING WINE, WHITE WINE AND PUDDING WINE.
HOW DO I KEEP EVERYTHING COOL?

A The sparkling and pudding wine are bound to be finished quickly after opening, so no problem there. If you plan on opening several dry whites, invest in an ice bucket, fill it with cubes and stick the bottles in there, within easy reach. Keep a tea towel ready for drips when serving.

Q SHOULD I FILL WINE GLASSES UP TO THE BRIM?

A No, one-third up is best. That way you can swirl the glass to release the aroma of the wine, which definitely adds to a wine's appeal.

3

In the summertime, the drinks, like the livin', should be easy. But they should also be interesting, fun and tasty, too. A tall order? Not after you've read this chapter, which gives loads of tips on the right wines, cocktails, soft drinks and beers to see you through some hot parties.

THE LOWDOWN

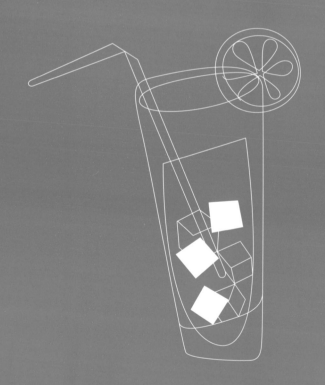

The temperature is starting to soar and lazy summer weekends stretch out in front of us. What better time for a party? It's wonderful to enjoy drinks outside, under the summer sun, sipping a delicious cocktail or glass of crisp, cool wine.

The best wines for the occasion are lighter, subtler and more elegant than in the winter. These will be the bottles that match hot-weather cuisine – salads, fish, seafood and barbecues. Don't forget chilled dry sherries, pink wines and sparklers, which all come into their own at summer parties. Reds need to be light and juicy. Read on about hot-weather wines later in this chapter.

Then there are cocktails, particularly frozen and fruity ones, which suit summer drinking. Here you'll find some new ideas, as well as a handy cross-reference to cocktails that appear throughout the book, which are guaranteed to go down well on high days and holidays.

Don't forget soft drinks. Now, more than any other time, it's crucial to provide plenty of inspiring non-alcoholic drinks. Even those who want a glass or two of wine or a cocktail may well turn to soft drinks before the party is over. Hot-weather drinking dehydrates, which isn't a great way to make your party swing, so be sure to look up the soft ideas offered here before your guests pass out in the heat!

THE Kit

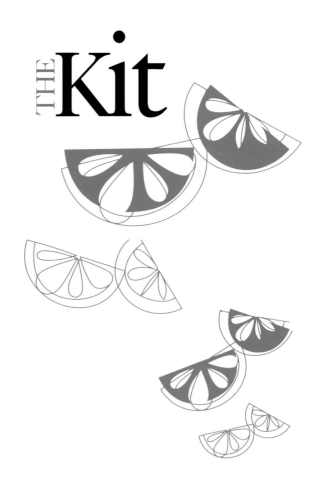

Feeling fruity – Here's a chance to let your imagination go wild as all the wonderful fresh fruit in the shops (or in your garden) comes into season. Fresh berries, like sprigs of redcurrants or individual raspberries, can be used to make drinks or garnish them. Slice into the bottom of a small strawberry and balance it on the side of a glass or use wedges of kiwi fruit in the same way.

Frozen fruit – Make fruit ice cubes to pop into drinks by freezing an individual raspberry or strawberry (or anything else that takes your fancy) with water in ice cube trays. Or simply freeze the fruit without water – frozen baby gooseberries and frosty green grapes are nice.

Flowers – Use tiny sprigs of little white flowers – hawthorn or elderflower, perhaps – to garnish drinks. Shake them hard and wash them to remove any insects, though! Or float single petals from larger flowers, like roses, in your drinks.

Fancy finery – Twiddly straws, gorgeous tumblers, sugar-rimmed glasses – this is the moment to use them.

Cooling kit – Stock up on ice, ice buckets, frozen sleeves that go over wine bottles (for cooling wine rapidly) and Thermos flasks (in case of taking cold drinks away from home, including iced tea and coffee).

Summer Wines

Ditch the rich, powerful wine styles of winter and think **light**, **crisp** and **easy-drinking**. The best summer whites are **deeply refreshing** and **mouthwatering**. They should have fresh, tangy acidity and light, fruity flavours – oaky whites like New World Chardonnays will taste too strong. Reds should be **juicy**, **soft** and **smooth**, not heavy and tannic. Choose:

—**Whites** – Sauvignon Blanc (from anywhere), Riesling (ditto), Muscadet (France), Soave, Frascati and Pinot Grigio (Italy), vin de pays des Côtes de Gascogne (France), dry/off-dry Chenin Blanc (France's Loire Valley or South Africa), unoaked Chardonnay (from anywhere), English dry whites, Picpoul de Pinet (France), Grüner Veltliner (Austria). Don't forget dry sherries, too. Fino and manzanilla are the styles to go for, served cold straight from the fridge.

—**Reds** – soft, easy Pinot Noir (from anywhere), Beaujolais and other Gamays (France), inexpensive lighter Merlot (anywhere), Tarrango (Australia), Cabernet Franc (Loire Valley), Bardolino, Valpolicella and other smooth Italian reds.

The only time to make an exception to the 'light wines' rule is for a barbecue! Barbie food has rich, strong flavours and textures — think smokey, char-grilled meat, oozing sweet red barbecue sauce, mustard and relish. On this occasion, bring out **very fruity**, **ripe wines**, probably from warm-climate vineyards in **Australia**, **South Africa** or **California**. For a white, try a buttery **Aussie Semillon-Chardonnay blend** and for a red, plump for a **ripe South African Pinotage**. Aim for rich flavours but not heavy tannins.

Alternatively, go for a **rosé** – the ultimate al-fresco summer drink – which is right back in fashion thanks to the new wave of fresh, modern pinks. Pick a **light**, **pale rosé** when drinking it on its own or with salads, cold meat or seafood. Choose a **deep cerise**, **gutsy rosé** with higher alcohol levels when lighting the barbie.

Sparkling wine is great for summer parties. It doesn't have to be Champagne. For big outdoor gatherings, pick a **light**, **dry cava** or an **English sparkler**. England now makes some smashing fizz; its crisp, aromatic style works well in hot weather. Don't forget to think about **pink fizz** for summer celebrations. Choose 'brut' (dry) styles.

Pick summer wines with **screw caps** to avoid the nasty mustiness that natural cork can occasionally give a wine. It's also convenient when you're on a picnic or out in the garden – simply unscrew your wine and reseal the bottle between servings to stop the wasps getting in. Plenty of good-quality wines now have screw caps.

Be inventive about summer wines. Try:

— **Kir and Kir Royale** – Cold **light**, **dry white wine** with a splash of **crème de cassis**. Use **sparkling wine** for Kir Royales. Add a shot of **vodka** for extra kick, if needed.

— **Spritzers** – Mix a simple, **tangy**, **unoaked white wine**, like Pinot Grigio, with good **fizzy water**, **ice** and slices of **citrus fruit**. Add a dash of **elderflower cordial** or **lime juice**, too. Or garnish with **chilled fresh fruit** – small green grapes, redcurrant sprigs or perhaps little baby gooseberries.

— **Chilled reds** – Serve summer reds **lightly chilled** to bring out their tangy, juicy quality. Keep in an ice bucket outside in hot weather. Or make SANGRIA by mixing chilled **light red wine** with **orange juice** and **pieces of fruit**, perhaps adding a shot of **brandy**, **grenadine** or even **crème de cassis** to liven things up.

—**Dry wine lovers** – Try mixing a shot of the bitter vermouth **Campari** into cold **dry, unoaked white wine**, then top up with fresh, chilled **sparkling water**, a slice of **lemon** and a little **ice**.

—**Sweet wine lovers** – Make a PEACH SHAKE, adapted from the lovely book *Al Fresco* (Ebury Press, 1991). To serve four: Blend 300ml **sweet white wine**, such as Muscat de Beaumes de Venise, with 6 ripe **peaches**, peeled, pitted and chopped, and 6 tablespoons **icing sugar**. Pour into Champagne flutes over crushed ice and decorate with little white flowers, if available.

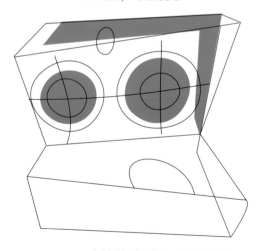

Summer Cocktails

Summer cocktails should be refreshing, fairly light and either fruity or minty. Obviously, this is the time of year when frozen cocktails (usually made with lots of crushed ice blended in) come into their own.

Make **Frozen Strawberry Daiquiris** (see page 18) or use another seasonal fruit. Garnish with a piece of the fresh fruit, such as a sliced strawberry, stuck on the side of the glass. Or try **Frozen Margaritas** (see page 21 for a basic recipe) made with the summery flavour of your choice– try it with apples, mangos, watermelons or whatever quenches your guests' thirst!

Try the classic and extremely refreshing MINT JULEP, a rather glamorous speciality of the state of Kentucky and made, of course, with the local Kentucky bourbon whiskey. Pack a tall glass two-thirds full with **crushed ice**, add 90ml **bourbon whiskey** and 30ml **sugar syrup**. Stir, top up with more ice. Garnish with **fresh mint sprigs**. (I like to swoosh the mint around or even squash it slightly before using so it releases more flavour.)

Limes are quintessentially summery. Mix fresh **lime juice** and **sugar syrup** to taste with a large shot of **citron vodka** and a dash of vivid **Galliano**. Serve in chilled martini glasses, rubbing the rims with lime wedges and dipping in caster sugar.

More ideas for cocktails that suit the summer mood can be found in other parts of this book: try the **Bellini** (page 99), the **Mojito** (page 122), the **Caipirinha** (page 122), the **Margarita** (page 21) and the **Gin Fizz** (page 19).

And that's not all. There are loads and loads of summery drinks, some very simple but effective. Make **icy cold**, **long vodkas** with **lime juice** and **tonic** or use **sloe gin** (make it yourself by steeping sloe berries in gin or buy Plymouth Sloe Gin) as the base for a late-summer **G'n'T**. Alternatively, add **lemonade** or **tonic** to cold **white port** (keep it in the fridge) and enjoy with some salty almonds for an authentic drink taken by port shippers working in the hot Douro Valley of Portugal.

Who could forget **Pimm's** and **lemonade** served with plenty of **apple**, thin slices of **cucumber** and **citrus fruits**, then garnished with **mint leaves**? Try adding a few drops of **bitters** or a splash of **grenadine** for extra whizz. Try **Campari**, too – this bitter vermouth is especially good in high summer with **grapefruit juice**.

For soft drinks, there's **homemade lemonade** or **limeade** made simply with **unwaxed fruit**, **water**, **sugar** and a little **citric acid**. Or splash out on real **old-fashioned, peppery ginger beer**, available in delis, and **elderflower syrup**.

Why not make ELDERFLOWER SYRUP yourself? Steep 20 **heads of elderflowers** in 1 litre **hot water** with 2 kilos **sugar** melted into it. Add 40g **citric acid**, the rind of 2 **lemons** and leave for 24 hours. Strain and store in the fridge, diluting with water to taste (or try with gin and mineral water).

Or use the Elderflower Syrup to make GINGER AND ELDERFLOWER CORDIAL. Grate a small piece of **root ginger** into a shaker or large jug with plenty of **elderflower syrup**, a dash of **lime juice** and **sparkling water**. Strain into glasses of **crushed ice** and garnish with **lime wedges**.

Alternatively, buy **white or wheat beer** made in Germany and Belgium. These cloudy, lemony beers are delicious served cold out of big jugs with lemon slices in the summer. Or try frothy **Belgian fruit beers**, especially cherry-flavoured Kriek. As always, serve well chilled.

And finally, don't forget iced tea and coffee. Make **iced tea**, perhaps with **Chai** (Indian spiced tea), or add **crushed mint leaves** and **sugar** to ordinary **black tea**. Mix a little **vanilla ice cream** into your **iced coffee** for a treat.

Party On...

🔍 I'M HAVING A BIG SUMMER DRINKS PARTY. HOW ON EARTH DO I KEEP EVERYTHING COLD?

🅰 Use every means at your disposal as it really is essential to keep all summer drinks cool. First, buy loads of ice along with your drinks and glass hire. Grab some big containers (clean plastic bins, old baths – use your imagination!) and place in the shade. Fill with ice and push your wine, beer and soft drink bottles into it. Also use ice buckets, freezer sleeves that fit over bottles, or even dangle bottles in a river, stream or paddling pool. Rather than getting in a sweat, make your cool drinks fun – and a talking point!

🔍 CAN I SERVE MY GUESTS WITH PLASTIC CUPS?

🅰 If you must. It is safer and more convenient when people are running around outside, perhaps by a pool. But ordinary plastic glasses certainly aren't sophisticated and they can have a slight synthetic odour. If you are going to avoid glass, perhaps go for pretty paper cups, instead.

Q I CAN'T KEEP OPENING BOTTLES OF WINE AND BEER AND DASHING
AROUND SERVING PEOPLE – I'LL MISS MY OWN PARTY!

A Outdoors summer parties are, by their very nature, supposed to be relaxed affairs. Buy wines with screw caps so you don't need a corkscrew, make sure you've got lots of glasses, napkins and so on to hand outside. Don't serve people; it looks too formal, anyway. Let your guests help themselves to the lot. Only make complicated cocktails at small parties.

Q WON'T MY WINE AND OTHER DRINKS ATTRACT LOTS OF WASPS? HOW CAN I KEEP THE BUGS AT BAY?

A Good point. No one wants a drowning wasp to garnish their cocktail! It is another good reason to choose bottles – especially wine – with screw caps as they are easier to reseal between servings. So, keep a lid on it or otherwise take a tip from mother and gently throw clean tea towels, netting or cake covers over bottles and jugs.

4
Christmas, New Year and Thanksgiving

Bring on the great big family party, held in the late autumn or winter, where the main focus is on warming food and plenty of cheering drinks. But which drinks? Although some of the oldest Yuletide ideas remain the best, drinks certainly don't have to be traditional at this time of year – the highly innovative and original can capture the spirit of the moment equally well. Here's a close look at the best styles of party drink to get you through the winter celebrations…

THE LOWDOWN

When the nights grow longer and the days get chillier, we crave richer, more intensely flavoured, spicier concoctions. The best wines are powerful, robust, full-bodied, whilst the best spirits are brown, not white, with long drinks spiced up with gingery, peppery or creamy hints. It doesn't matter that some winter drinks are served cold, as long as they taste rich and robust.

Winter warmers, in short, are guaranteed to soothe the soul. Perhaps the very best of all are the hot, steamy comfort drinks – mulls, punches and toddies – whether alcoholic or not. These are party drinks to fuel a chilly gathering.

So here is a selection to warm the cockles. Here are the best drinks for winter dinners, for fiery cocktails, for after-dinner musings by the fire and for festive winter parties from Hallowe'en and Thanksgiving to Christmas and New Year.

64 **Glasses** – Have fun serving winter drinks in interesting vessels. Big, **chunky tumblers** come in handy for pouring spirits either straight or 'on the rocks'. Forget small, old-fashioned schooners for liqueurs, port and sherry – they're just too little – and instead use larger glasses; **ordinary wine glasses** are just fine. You'll need **cocktail glasses** if you are attempting the ideas on pages 12–24 and tall, thin **champagne flutes** for fizz. Finally, try to find some **thick glass mugs** with metal holders for hot mulls – they look just right. If not, use chunky wine glasses, not delicate ones.

Fruit, spices and chocolate – Make sure you have everything you need to garnish and decorate your winter drinks, as well as to make a good spiced mull: **nutmeg**, **cloves** and **cinnamon sticks** are a must. Buy new spices if you only have ancient ones, as they do lose their aromas and flavours over time. You might find **mace**, **cocoa powder**, **cinnamon powder** and **ground ginger** useful, as well as **citrus fruit** and **apples** for mulls. Buy organic, unwaxed fruit whenever possible. Stock up on **vanilla pods**, **chilli peppers**, **dried herbs** and any other ingredient for infusing, as well as **sugar** and **brandy** for mulled wine. **Coffee**, **cream**, **whisky** and **grated chocolate**, as well as sticks of **flaky chocolate** and **marshmallows**, are all useful for after-dinner liqueur coffees.

Infusions – Play around with the ideas you find here to make original drinks,
perhaps using homemade infusions. Try soaking **vanilla pods** or **chilli peppers**
for a week or two in **vodka** for a wonderfully aromatic spirit. Or what about
coffee beans in **white rum**? Or **dried thyme** in **sugar syrup**? Or **maraschino
cherries** in **Spanish brandy**? Come up with your own ideas. Don't forget,
anything you can make well in advance, such as infused spirits, saves time on
the day and will impress the folks no end!

Decorations – Winter feasts and parties can take a lot of decorating before
they look naff, so bring on the accessories! Get out a posh **decanter**, polish the
wooden coasters, tie **velvet ribbon** or **holly sprigs** round your mulled wine
glasses, stick a piece of **cinnamon** in the mug, add **gold ribbon** to anything.
Go for it, especially at Christmas, which can be played up as much as you like.

winter cocktails

Cocktails in the winter months should be one of two things: either **soothing** and **comforting** – in which case, think sweet, creamy flavours – or **warming** and **exciting** – think fiery, spicy, gingery. Get away completely from the tart, tangy, light 'n' frothy summer styles. This is not the moment to make Frozen Strawberry Daiquiris!

Beware over-sugary, creamy cocktails, especially at a party, when you probably want to drink more than one. Thick alcoholic gloop is too cloying to knock back in any quantity. Think subtle.

• If you must have a creamy cocktail, make it a cool, stylish one such as a BRANDY ALEXANDER. Pour 50ml **Cognac**, 20ml **brown crème de cacao**, 15ml **double cream** into a shaker with ice. Shake, strain into a chilled cocktail glass and grate some **fresh nutmeg** on top to garnish.

• Or make your own with **vodka** infused with real **vanilla pods** and **coffee beans**.
Then mix with **milk**, **cream** and **Kahlua**. Sprinkle aromatic **cinnamon** on top.

• Brown spirits – whisky, brandy, rum – provide the best base for winter cocktails
as they have aptly rich, spicy, woody flavours. Try a whisky-based cocktail for
some smokey depths, such as HORSE'S NECK. Pour 50ml **bourbon whiskey** into
a highball glass with plenty of **ice**, top up with **ginger ale** and garnish with a
long spiral of **lemon peel**, draped over the edge of the glass. Classy; easy.

• Guinness and Champagne sounds so unlikely, yet a BLACK VELVET is a
wonderful blend of the elegant and fresh with the smooth and earthy. Take a
champagne flute, half-fill with **Guinness** and slowly top up with 'brut'
Champagne (or dry cava). The classic recipe for a **Champagne Cocktail** is great
on New Year's Eve (see page 16).

• Experiment with warming, fiery, full-flavoured cocktail ingredients to your
heart's content: appley, autumnal **Calvados**; pruney **Armagnac**; herbal, medicinal
liqueurs like **Chartreuse** and **Benedictine**; dark, raisiny **rums**; orangey-rich
Cointreau and **Grand Marnier**.

warming
MULLs
& HOT
toddies

What could be better at
an autumn or winter gathering
than a hot, alcoholic cup of
spiced wine? It doesn't even
have to be wine, so how about
warmed cider, port or cranberry
cordial? Here's how to do it…

Mull 1 – Red Wine

Forget powder mixes, spice bags and so on. Make your own mulled red wine – it's extremely easy and much more reliable if you take control of what goes in the pot! Respect your mull: use a decent, **medium-bodied**, **fruity red wine** rather than nasty cheap plonk. Warm up a bottle's-worth of wine gently in a big pan with a few **cloves**, a **cinnamon stick**, some slices of **orange** and **lemon**, a little **sugar** and a slug of fine **brandy**. The quantities are up to you – add a little spice, citrus peel, sugar and brandy to start with and build up, to taste. Make sure all the ingredients are fresh, including the cloves. Go easy on the cloves – they can release a very strong, almost medicinal oil if left to stew. Heat, *not* boil, the mull (as you can get an unpleasant jammy, cooked flavour and a distinct lack of alcohol if it steams off into the night). Serve in big, thick glass cups if at all possible, or ordinary red wine glasses.

Mull 2 – Cider Cup

Use good-quality, still or gently frothy **farmhouse cider**, not the violently fizzy, commercial stuff. Add **sugar** to **dry cider**, but not to sweet. Use **apple** pieces as well as **citrus slices**, more **cinnamon** and less **cloves** than for wine, and a dash of **Calvados** instead of ordinary brandy.

Mull it over – more ideas:

• Try a mixture of **red port** and **red wine** as the base – strong, but most definitely warming.

• **White wine** can be used – ideally, choose a **fruity**, **unoaked**, **slightly off-dry white**, perhaps South African Chenin Blanc.

• Hot **honeyed mead** is another idea, often sold in rural spots around the UK. Heat up and add your **spices** and **brandy** to taste (but hold the sugar).

• Or what about a traditional **wassail cup** at Christmas? Ancient English recipes call for equal measures of **brown ale** and **cider**, heated with some **spices** (mace, cinnamon sticks, grated ginger, nutmeg), strained, and poured over small **eating apples** which have been cored, sprinkled with **sugar** and baked in a hot oven until tender. Serve the lot, apples and all, from a punchbowl or huge pan. Very 'Ye Olde Yuletide' and bound to be a talking point!

• For a **non-alcoholic punch**, warm up **cranberry** or **red grape juice** or a blend of the two with **spices**, such as star anise, cinnamon and cloves, and perhaps a slice of fresh **root ginger**. I have successfully used the inky-purple juice of ordinary hedgerow **blackberries** as the base for a child-friendly Hallowe'en witches' potion, too. Add **spices**, **dried cranberries**, plenty of **sugar**, **rubber spiders**…

Hot toddies

Hot toddies are a cheerful idea for gatherings on very cold winter days – shooting parties, queues for winter sales, waiting outside rock concerts, picket lines – wherever you can take a Thermos. The best base is **Irish potcheen**, now available under licence sometimes, mainly in tourist and duty-free shops in Ireland. Otherwise, use **Irish whiskey**. Put a shot of **whiskey** in a mug, top up with **hot water**, add a couple of **cloves**, some **brown sugar** and bingo. It drives away the cold like nothing else.

The food and drinks writer Michael Van Straten, best known for his healthy drinks recipes, has a lovely soothing non-alcoholic tea that would suit a winter afternoon party: MARMALADE AND GINGER TEA. Grate 1cm **fresh root ginger**, place it in a mug and top up with **boiling water**. Leave for five minutes. Strain, then add 1 tablespoon of organic, **thin-cut orange marmalade** and stir until dissolved. (Sounds positively life-saving. You could add a shot of **golden** or **dark rum** and serve with dark ginger cake, of course.)

BROWN Spirits

Brown spirits are especially suitable for winter drinking because of their rich, smokey-spicy depths and darker colours. For parties, serve as long drinks (add soda, ginger ale, cola, anything you like…) or use them to make cocktails. At the end of a dinner party, serve on their own or with ice, while chatting by the fire.

Whisky – It's hard to think of a drink that suits the winter more than whisky. Malt whisky – the great spirit of Scotland – is made from malted barley, often dried over a peat fire, plus local water and yeast. It's distilled twice and aged in barrels, which adds flavour and colour. Single malt is the product of one distillery; blended whisky is from several distilleries, made from wheat or corn and barley. Try:

—**Single malt** from the Islands, especially Islay, for its peaty-smokey character

—**American whiskey**, sweeter and more mellow, with a slightly charred flavour, from Tennessee or Kentucky

—**Irish whiskey**, triple distilled for extra smoothness and purity

—**Blended whisky** mixed with ginger wine

Rum – A versatile and hedonistic party drink, and not just for drunken sailors.
White rum is unaged and a bit boring, but okay for mixing. Gold rums are aged in casks to take on spicy, orangey notes. Dark rums are rich and raisiny, much more exciting. Rum is made from either molasses or sugar cane. Try rums from:

— **Barbados** – mellow and classy

— **Cuba** – one authentic Cuban brand – Havana Club – dominates

— **Guyana** – some of the best and most complex around

— **Jamaica** – a wide range, mainly quite powerful in style

— and… **Daiquiris** – the classic rum-based cocktail (see page 18)

Brandy – Made from clear grape spirit, brandy is aged in oak barrels for years until it picks up a deep amber colour and mellow flavours from the wood. The most famous brandies are made in the Cognac and Armagnac regions of France. Also try:

— **Brandy de Jerez**, from southern Spain, sweeter, smoother, almost toffee-like

— **Fruit brandies**, especially **Calvados**, made from apples in Normandy

— **Brandy** and **lemonade**, surprisingly refreshing!

TABLE WINES

Planning a big Christmas or Thanksgiving get-together? Both these traditional celebrations involve eating a huge amount of food, and probably sitting down with a vast number of relations to do so. Wine is the order of the day, then, as it is the best drink for matching with food. And with the sort of rich feast that marks such occasions, you'll need fairly **full-on, powerful wines**.

Weedy, light, summery wines are out. Think of a plate groaning with turkey, gravy, spuds and other vegetables, not to mention the sauces, peppery stuffing and other trimmings. The best bet to wash down this lot is **very fruity, ripe wine**. If you're feeding and watering a crowd, rest assured the perfect bottles are not necessarily the most expensive. **Smooth, easy-drinking reds** and **juicy, ripe whites** from warmer, new-wave wine countries like Australia, Chile and California hit the mark perfectly.

Happily, both whites and reds go with the classic roast bird, as long as they are rich and fruity. Reds: plump for **Shiraz-Cabernet** blends from Oz; **Cabernet** or **Merlot** from Chile or **red Zinfandel** from California. Or **red Rioja** from Spain — pick an older one, perhaps. The ideal white is the generously fruity **Chardonnay** grape. Don't forget a **sweet wine** with dessert (and especially with Christmas pud). Sweet, sparkling **Asti** is a light, refreshing choice.

A similar rule applies to any winter party where you want to drink wine. Ignore the lighter, crisper styles that suit summer so well, and pick **rounded, fruity, ripe bottles** from warm-climate areas. Slightly **spicy, peppery reds** from the Rhône Valley are good bets for beating a chill; peachy, lively **Viognier** from France or elsewhere makes a nice change from Chardonnay.

For New Year's Eve, a **sparkling wine** is a must. Although **Champagne** is often fabulous (see page 96–7), it's fine to go with **Spanish cava** or a **New World fizz**, perhaps from New Zealand, where the bubblies really shine. Or dare to be different and pop open an **Australian sparkling Shiraz** — ruddy red, frothy and curranty — at midnight. Groovy, baby!

AFTER DINNER DRINKS

If winter is the ideal time for hot punches, spicy cocktails and rich red wines, it is also the best moment for sipping an after-dinner drink, ideally in front of a roaring fire, listening to mellow music and putting the world to rights with your party guests. Don't forget the ritual is part of creating the right mood – bring a bottle out with the glasses on a tray and pour in front of your guests. To keep warm while chilling out, try the following:

— **Port** – the classic fortified red wine made in Northern Portugal. Go for red port in the form of good-value **LBV** (late-bottled vintage) or super-smart **vintage** (made in exceptionally good years only); or try **tawny** port, which is aged in oak cask until brown, nutty and spicy. Serve in wine glasses with nuts, chocolate, raisins or pieces of full-flavoured hard cheese

—**Madeira** – another fortified wine, this time from the island of the same name. Under-rated, fine Madeira is wonderful, concentrated stuff with a really long, lingering nuts-and-raisin flavour. After dinner, try **malmsey**, the sweetest style of Madeira

—**Dessert wine** or **sweet sherry** – chill a fine pudding wine and serve it on its own so you can savour the complex flavours. Try a **Tokaji** from Hungary or a sweet **oloroso sherry** from Spain

—**Liqueur** – gradually creeping back into fashion. A liqueur is usually a sweet, spirit-based concoction made with a particular flavour such as herbs, fruit or nuts. Some nasty, sickly ones lurk out there, but there are some which are fascinating, rare creatures. Try **Benedictine** or **Chartreuse** (herby); **Grand Marnier** (orangey) or the wonderful Spanish **Pacharan** (sloes and anise)

—**Brown spirits** – see pages 72–3 for the lowdown on brown spirits to sip after dinner, all on their own

—**Irish coffee** – made with **whipped cream** and **Irish whiskey**. Or ring the changes with **rum**, or **Cognac**. Use only high-quality ingredients – fine, newly made coffee, fresh cream, top spirits. Grate chocolate on top and consider marshmallows…

THE PERFECT HOST
TIPS

🍷 SOME OF THE DRINKS DESCRIBED HERE – THE QUALITY BROWN SPIRITS AND EXOTIC LIQUEURS – SOUND EXPENSIVE. ARE THEY?

🅰 A few are, but here's the good news. Because they generally have rich, concentrated flavours, they should go a very long way. Buy a bottle of, say, Chartreuse or a fine single malt, and you only need serve small quantities as the character of the drink is so intense. That goes for cocktail ingredients, too. The spirits and liqueurs should last for months after opening, so you can enjoy them well into the new year.

🍷 I'VE GOT LOTS OF CHILDREN, DRIVERS AND TEETOTALLERS COMING IN OVER CHRISTMAS. CAN YOU SUGGEST ANY NON-ALCOHOLIC DRINKS?

🅰 Family parties always mean more non-drinkers than usual! Stock up on interesting soft drinks, such as cranberry cordial, ginger beer and exotic juices, like the newly fashionable pomegranate. Ideas for more complex soft drinks are on pages 56–7. Avoid the 'orange juice' cliché.

🍷 I'D LIKE TO TREAT MY GUESTS TO A VERY SPECIAL WINE FOR CHRISTMAS
OR THANKSGIVING THIS YEAR. CAN YOU SUGGEST A SUBLIME RED THAT GOES
WITH TURKEY?

🅰 With pleasure! Impress your wine buff friends by opening a mature claret
(red Bordeaux) from a very good vintage (check in a pocket guide, or ask a
trusted merchant). Choose a Cabernet-heavy wine from the Médoc part of
Bordeaux, decant it before serving to air it and enjoy. If you want a posh white,
make it a top-notch white Burgundy (100% Chardonnay, from the region that can
produce the very best examples).

🍷 I'D LIKE TO SERVE SPARKLING WINE ON NEW YEAR'S EVE, BUT MANY
OF MY GUESTS COMPLAIN IT IS TOO DRY AND ACIDIC. HAVE YOU GOT
ANY SOLUTIONS?

🅰 Most Champagne and sparkling wine sold is 'brut' (dry) and has a distinctly
crisp, mouthwatering finish. Although lots of us love it, other people might prefer
an off-dry sparkler – look out for the words 'demi-sec' on the label instead of
'brut' for a slightly sweeter, richer style.

5 Girls' and Boys' parties

Planning a girlie night out – perhaps a hen party – or a boys-only night on the town? It's easy to let everyone get stuck in separately at the bar, ordering their own individual drinks, but the host with the most will plan drinks that are more organised and sociable – ordering a particular cocktail by the jug, perhaps, deciding on Champagne or other fizz for the group all night, or planning a late-night single malt tasting. Make the drinks an essential part of the party, the thing that pulls everyone together.

THE LOWDOWN

Just a generation ago, it was one drink for the ladies and another for the men; girls sipped either a bland, off-dry German white or gin 'n' tonic while boys downed a beer, red wine or whisky instead. Step back a further generation and the gulf was even wider – pink vermouth, cherry liqueur or (yeuch) Advocaat for the women; scotch on the rocks or bottles of brown ale for the men. Only cocktails bridged the gap (read *The Great Gatsby* for tales of men and women drinking cocktails together in the Roaring Twenties).

Thank goodness all this has now changed and anyone can drink whatever they like. Usually, that means ordering a round of beers or a bottle or two of wine and sharing it, regardless of gender. Apart from the fact that women have to be more careful about the amount they drink (sorry, girls, it is a simple biological fact that our bodies do not process alcohol as well as men's do), anything goes. Don't let a pompous bore tell you otherwise, let alone order for you!

That said, there are two exceptions. I'm talking about the hen night (or girls-only evening) and the stag night (or boys' night on the town). Somehow, at these moments, it is fun to slip into stereotypes once more – ironically, of course! So here are some fun suggestions on how to *vive la différence*, drinks-wise.

g*i*Rls' *parties*

Clearly you wouldn't want to get all pink and fluffy, silly and naff on a hen night, would you? Well, of course you would! This is exactly the moment to bring out some of the most camp, lurid drinks of all (unless you can afford to drink classy Champagne cocktails all night).

So, ditch the boring spritzers, dull white wines and bland lagers. They aren't fun enough, they aren't flavoursome enough and they most definitely do not make a statement! It's a girls' night out, so go for it! Choose something fizzy, something colourful or something mixed – preferably the latter, in the form of a wild cocktail.

Pick a drink that is really easy and swift for the bar to put together. What about the remarkably simple but wonderfully frivolous **Woo Woo**? I've given the recipe here just in case you want to try it at home, but out on the town someone else will be doing the mixing.

WOO WOO Pour equal amounts of **peach schnapps** and **vodka**, plus **cranberry** **juice** to taste, into tall tumblers with lots of **ice** in them. Stir and serve immediately. This is one cocktail that you can make a little in advance, and which could be blended by the jugful.

This drink really seems to suit the girls – you don't catch many stag night parties hitting the **Woo Woos**, anyway. But if sweet peach schnapps isn't your thing, try a **Sea Breeze** instead, which is drier (and a bit more sophisticated, to be honest).

SEA BREEZE Pour equal measures of **vodka** and **cranberry juice,** plus half the amount of **grapefruit juice**, into a cocktail shaker with **ice**. Shake and strain into tall tumblers. Can be made in large quantities a little in advance.

Then there's the ultimately girly **Piña Colada**. Very retro, this cocktail. For some reason, it always makes me think of Wham! So camp it up, garnishing with garish paper umbrellas, pineapple slices, maraschino cherries. Oh, and do respect all those rich ingredients and take it easy when drinking this…

PIÑA COLADA Mix 30ml **white rum**, 50ml **pineapple juice** and 20ml **tinned coconut cream** with **crushed ice** and pour into tall tumblers. Top up with 15ml **gold rum**.

If you want wine, avoid bland, weedy whites (very cheap Italian or French wines), heavily oaked numbers (Chardonnays and perhaps Viogniers); medium-dry sugary whites (poor German styles like Liebfräumilch); old rosés; powerful tannic reds. All are bound to disappoint.

Instead, try wines with more life and flavour, such as **sprightly, refreshing, tangy whites** like **Sauvignon Blanc**; **dry Riesling** (perhaps from Australia); young, lively **modern rosés** (from France, California or Spain); **unoaked Chardonnays** and **lighter reds** (which can be slightly chilled). Dry, succulent, chilled **fino sherry** is a newly trendy and deeply refreshing choice, usually found in tapas bars; and you can't go wrong with decent **dry fizz**.

Finally, a warning: She who downs masses of cream liqueur on a big night out with the girls will live to regret it. Or just not live.

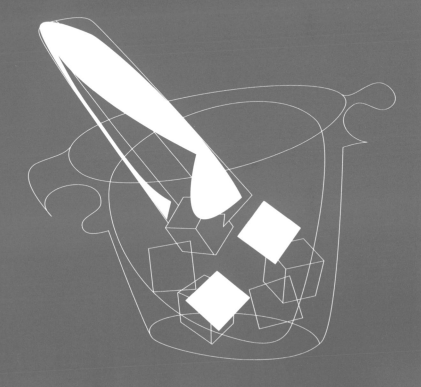

GIRLS' AND BOYS' PARTIES

Boy, is it hard to give men advice on stag-night drinking. They just won't be told. But a few guidelines from a mate might go down okay, so do read on, best man-to-be…

Simple fact: You will get a much better pint by turning your back on bland mass-market lager (usually American) and going for **real English ale** or interesting **Belgian**, **German** or **Czech beers** instead. These will bring bags more flavour, a lot more complexity and satisfaction, and quite probably a bit less alcohol. Which, if you're boozing all night, is A Good Thing. Honest.

So, wave goodbye to gassy, boring, over-hyped branded lagers, then, and instead opt for:

- **Real ale: the local brew** – ale made in a micro-brewery up the road will almost certainly taste fresh and good. It's great to support these producers, too.

- **Wheat or white beer** – Bavarian or Belgian, preferably.

- **Stout or Porter** – dark, rich, Irish/London beers, respectively. Yes, they are fattening, and yes, they can give you gut-rot if you drink too much, but they taste sensational, and anyway, it's a *boys' night out*…

- **Aussie sparkling ale** – refreshing stuff, crisp and lightish with yeasty flavours from a second fermentation in the bottle. Cool choice, in every sense.

- **Czech lager** – anyone who has been to Prague knows. High-quality. Order it by the jug – more sociable.

- **Farmhouse cider** – not the unnaturally orange, fiercely fizzy mass-market stuff, but real cider made, preferably, at the local farm. Strong and tasty.

Later on, you might settle down to a few 'straighteners' (or 'stiffeners', if you please). This usually means a shot of fine **single malt whisky**, although someone in the group might prefer **bourbon** or **Cognac**, something rather suave and masculine, naturally. See pages 72–3 for the lowdown on brown spirits. Avoid the cheapest blended whiskies or rubbish French brandies even if the pockets feel empty and you no longer care much what you drink. Trade up and you will taste the difference and you will feel better for it the next day! Alternatively, crack open a really good bottle of **port** (see page 76).

Finally, if you had a little too much fun trying out these ideas, turn rapidly to Chapter 9 the very second you wake up the next day.

Boys' night out

THE PERFECT HOST
TIPS

Q BUT WE ALL WANT DIFFERENT DRINKS – SURELY THAT'S OKAY?
A Of course it is, but it's more fun to get the drinks in together and order something that everyone can dip into. That means jugs of cocktails, a huge bucket of beer, magnums of fizz… It's simply a good party trick to order this way as it looks generous, is sociable, can be a talking point… and everyone can fill up from the table rather than waiting at the bar half the evening.

Q I'M DRIVING/PREGNANT/TEETOTAL – WHAT SHOULD I HAVE?
A There are loads of great soft drinks around (this book lists some on pages 56–7). Avoid non- or low-alcoholic wine or beer as it is often vile, and stick to proper soft drinks (juice or juice-based, gingery or sodas) instead. If you want a small dose of alcohol, try a wine that is naturally low in alcohol, like good German Riesling, which often comes in at just 7–10%, as opposed to 14.5% for some table wines.

Q IS THERE A GOLDEN RULE FOR AVOIDING HANGOVERS?

A Not one, but three – eat beforehand, pace yourself slowly and don't mix your drinks. Do all of these and you'll know when you've had enough (and maybe even stop).

Q ISN'T A BRIDE-/GROOM-TO-BE SUPPOSED TO GET TOTALLY HAMMERED? CAN WE SPIKE THEIR DRINKS?

A It isn't on to spike anyone's drink, ever. You never know what might go wrong. Ideally, one person should look out for the bride/groom all night, and make sure they have a fab time, keeping them topped up with something delicious, without over-doing it, making sure the drinks stay cold, fresh and constant. That person could be a nominated driver, perhaps. She/he will get their reward in heaven (or the very next day, from the grateful hen/stag!).

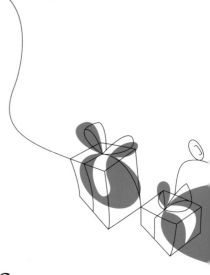

6 Weddings, Christenings and Birthday Parties

It's the big day – your wedding (or your daughter's), your 30th birthday, your baby's christening or your silver anniversary. Everyone is invited to the party and the caterers are sorted, but what about the drinks? There's plenty of pressure to get everything right… and you can, if you follow this guide to the best drinks for celebrations!

THE LOWDOWN

It's during life's great celebratory moments that I enjoy drinking most of all. Here are your closest friends and family, raising a glass to toast a really happy event – a wedding, a christening, a birthday – or to celebrate successful exam results, an engagement or a big anniversary. Whatever the occasion, these are the best parties of all, when you have something to make merry over, so the drinks should reflect this and be cheerful, life-affirming and gorgeous!

Of course, some of life's most important moments have particular drinking traditions. Christening teas are sometimes 'dry'. If high tea is the order of the day, splash out on a range of luxury teas and coffees, some herbal infusions and good quality soft drinks. Don't let instant coffee or grotty tea-bags rule the day!

Wedding receptions are, of course, inextricably linked to fizz (for an easy guide, see pages 96–7) although you might consider a traditional wedding cup for bride and groom (see page 100). Incidentally, did you know that the word 'toast' comes from an old tradition of soaking toast (or a crouton, if you are French) in a bowl of drink, which is passed around the guests for everyone to take a mouthful? The host is supposed to take the last sip and eat the toast. Yuck! Who wants a

sodden old piece of bread in a bowl that everyone has slurped from? Not me –
I don't like my friends THAT much…

Luckily, there are many more appealing ways to toast – and host – the really
special moments in life. Here they are, from the best fizz for accompanying
speeches and wines to go with a wedding feast, to the most celebratory of
cocktails, as well as suggestions for drinks that match party cakes to perfection.

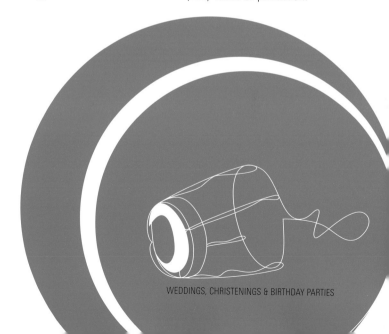

WEDDINGS, CHRISTENINGS & BIRTHDAY PARTIES

Weddings, christenings and birthdays are all celebrations that simply wouldn't be the same without joyful sparklers, which deliver lovely **teasing bubbles**, plenty of **fresh**, **crisp fruitiness** and a lovely **kick of alcohol**. (Sparkling wines are not necessarily stronger than non-sparkling wines, but the bubbles do mean the alcohol hits the bloodstream more quickly.)

Champagne is a wonderful option here. Not all sparkling wine is Champagne — champers comes only from the region of north-east France and no other bubbly can use the name. It is expensive stuff, so is Champagne worth it? It should be, if you buy cleverly. Choose from **vintage** (from one good year, named on the label) and **non-vintage** (blended from several different years). **Don't** splash out on pricey vintage and drink it too young — it can take several years to mellow and be at its best. **Do** buy older vintages if you want the very best in fizz. **Do** choose non-vintage from a reliable label and always taste before buying in bulk. **Avoid** cut-price, 'bargain' Champagne from an obscure label — it can be tart and bland.

LOVELY BUBBLY

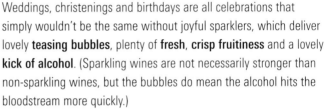

Champagne makes a statement and the top examples are dazzling, but if you have lots of guests you may well want to spend less. The good news is there's lots of choice:

• Still in **France**, but outside the Champagne region, try a **crémant** – the offical name given to the best sparklers from other parts of the country. **Crémant de Bourgogne** (Burgundy) is especially recommended

• **Cava** from **Spain** is a reliable, clean and fresh sparkler – and a genuine bargain

• Other countries tipped for their fruity, good-quality fizz are **New Zealand**, **Australia**, **California** and **England**

• Try **Italian Prosecco**, made near Venice, for a dry, elegant, fairly simple style of fizz at a reasonable price

For aperitif fizz, go for a label that says **'brut'** (dry). Consider serving **magnums** or even bigger bottles, as this looks generous and impressive. Don't forget **pink sparklers**, which can be romantic and celebratory. **Never** spray the fizz around, even if you are totally over-excited – this is not celebrating in style, it's wasting good wine and looks naff! **Chill** all bubbles before serving and be careful how you open the bottles, as the cork is under pressure and could explode in someone's face.

CELEBRATORY
COCKTAILS

The **Bellini** is, I reckon, a great cocktail for celebrations. It's soft and fruity, pulpy and slightly sweet. It's highly suitable for small gatherings, for birthdays and christenings, but perhaps too complex for big crowds.

BELLINI Put 30ml **chilled peach puree**, in a mixing jug and carefully top up with 90ml **cold dry sparkling wine** (try Prosecco). Don't stir or the fizz will go flat. Strain into champagne flutes and pour 15ml **peach liqueur** on top.

Alternatively, go for a **Champagne Cocktail** (see page 16). Why not use a Schnapps, called Goldschlager, which has fine gold leaf floating in it. A dash of this in a champagne flute topped up with fizz looks spectacular with tiny edible gold flakes dancing around in the bubbles. Or make **Kir Royales** (see page 52) with sparkling wine and crème de cassis, then float a fresh raspberry on top of each flute.

100   Traditional toasts

—To bring good luck during your marriage, try a traditional two-handled **wedding cup**. Originating from Germany in the fifteenth century, the idea is that the bride and groom drink out of the same cup without spilling a drop. It doesn't particularly matter what goes in the cup, but fizz might not be a good idea in case someone splutters and spills it! You can buy traditional wedding cups from various online wedding specialists.

—Try a **spiced wine**, especially at winter weddings. Norman folklore has it that around midnight, guests place a potion called Bride's Broth in the bedroom. I can find no recipe for this, but it must have been warm, aromatic, spicy and powerfully intoxicating. Try using **mulled wine** (see page 68), but add more brandy.

—**Mead** (a honeyed alcoholic drink) is a traditional drink for weddings and might be an interesting idea for an old-fashioned Medieval-style do. Buy in shops at historic tourist sites – usually old abbeys, Celtic monuments and so on.

Soft options

Don't forget to provide non-alcoholic drinks – plenty of **mineral water**, of course, but for celebrations, something appealing like **elderflower cordial** made up with **sparkling water** or **lemonade** so the non-drinkers get some celebratory fizz too. Alternatively, buy **pressés** – cranberry, lime and so on – that are already fizzy.

WEDDINGS, CHRISTENINGS & BIRTHDAY PARTIES

102

Wines for banquets

Fizz goes well with canapés and even with light starters, but if serving rich savoury dishes or even a hearty buffet, you will need fruitier, riper table wines capable of standing up to the flavours of the food. Avoid weak wines, instead choose those with plenty of soft, ripe fruit. Don't pick reds that are too tannic or heavy – they will not be terribly user-friendly at a party. Here some styles of wine that tend to be reliable and popular across a wide range of guests:

- **Chardonnay-Semillon** blends from **Australia** are fine with both chicken and pork

- **Cabernet-Shiraz** blends, also from **Australia**, work well with lamb and beef

- **Argentinian Malbec**, which has lots of ripe black cherry character, is excellent with red meat and savoury buffet food

- The **Pinot Noir** grape, from **France** or elsewhere, makes smooth, rounded, versatile reds that go with most savoury food, including chicken and even salmon

- **Rhône reds** – particularly the less expensive **Côtes-du-Rhône Villages** wines – are fruity and slightly spicy. Good with red meat casseroles

- Unoaked or lightly oaked **Chardonnays** are great with a wide range of food, from fish dishes (white fish and salmon) to creamy chicken

cake complements

It's simple: serve sweet drinks with sweet food! Make it proper **dessert wine**, too. I've been to wedding receptions where port was served (and hardly touched) or there was a bank of spirits sitting on a table after dinner (ditto). To interest your guests in something new, provide a **luscious honeyed wine** that actually goes with the pudding or the wedding cake. Bring out small **half-bottles** of good, chilled dessert wine (from **Bordeaux**, perhaps, or **Germany**) on every table and I guarantee your guests will appreciate it. Richer stickier sweet wines go best with fruitcakes (try **Australian Liqueur Muscat**).

It's the same at christenings and birthday parties. The best drink to serve with the cake is a sweet wine, and in this case preferably a **sweet, light sparkling wine**. The famous Italian sparkler, **Asti**, its more subtle, lightly frothy cousin, **Moscato d'Asti**, and the light, medium-sweet French **Clairette de Die**, are all great choices in this instance. Why? Because you get the 'pop' of a cork, plenty of bubbles in your glass and the honeyed sweetness of the wine, which goes well with all sweet celebration cakes, and especially creamy ones. Even better, the alcohol level is naturally low in these wines, so it is just enough to perk up your guests, but not enough to lay them out – which is just as well if you are going to keep on partying…

OPENING fiZZ AND THE PERFECT tOASt

Opening a bottle of bubbly and toasting a special occasion is the most formal, ceremonial moment in the world of drinks. Here are a few tips on how to get it absolutely right!

— **Make sure everyone's glass gets a top-up** directly before the speech. It feels pretty silly to toast a special moment with an empty glass. Pour each drink individually beside the guest rather than bringing in a tray of filled glasses, as the fizz will start to go flat and warm quickly.

—**Parade around with something really special** at this point, especially if it's in magnums. But don't mix it with another wine sitting in the bottom of the glasses. Either encourage guests to drink up or provide fresh glasses for a new wine.

—**Make sure the fizz is properly chilled**. It will taste better, and open more easily (and less explosively) when cold.

—**To open sparkling wine correctly**, carefully peel off the foil and wire cage, while keeping a hand over the cork. It can pop out with great force, so always point the bottle away from anyone's face. Now hold the main part of bottle firmly in one hand, and the top in the other, keeping it at an angle rather than straight up, and carefully, slowly, twist the cork out. Aim for a quiet 'pssht' noise rather than a loud bang, for minimum spills.

—**Pour down the side of the glass** (hold it at an angle) so it doesn't bubble up too fiercely, and top up once the froth has subsided.

—**Don't forget the non-drinkers**, as always. Sparkling elderflower cordial or old-fashioned lemonade are good soft options here.

—**After the (doubtless brilliant) speech**, make a clear point of asking your guests to raise their glasses, all together, to toast the occasion – and make the most of this lovely ritual!

THE PERFECT HOST
TIPS

Q ANY TIPS ON HOW TO BUY WINES IN BULK?

A If you have the time, it's lovely to visit a wine region and taste at a few cellar doors, picking your own wine and bringing it back in the car. It can be cost-effective and you get a nice break in wine country, too! But if time is short, and you are using a wine shop, there are three crucial rules. 1) Make sure you taste everything before committing to a bulk purchase (ask for free samples or buy a bottle of every contender and have a mini-tasting at home). 2) Buy sale or return so you can take back any unused stocks. 3) Get a decent discount for buying in large quantities. Reject any shop that can't satisfy these criteria.

Q WE ARE HOLDING A FAMILY PARTY IN A HOTEL WHICH INSISTS WE USE THEIR OWN WINE LIST. HOW DO WE CHOOSE FROM IT?

A Try asking what the 'corkage' charge is for bringing your own wine – it may be low. If the hotel still insists, then go by the same principles as above. They simply must let you taste through a few of their wines before the event, and they should offer a discount on their normal list price if you are going to get through a **109** lot. Bargain hard. Use the tips on restaurant wine lists on page 130.

Q ANY HINTS FOR THE PERFECT TOAST?
A I would buy fairly inexpensive wine for the main part of the evening, but splash out on something truly memorable to give guests a glass each during the speeches and toasts. Tell them to empty their glasses and then get the waiters to parade in with magnums of Champagne and dispense a glassful each. This is the moment to show off! You can always go back to discount cava afterwards.

Q HOW SHOULD LANDMARK BIRTHDAYS BE CELEBRATED, DRINKSWISE?
A Always tailor the drink to the person and their age group. At 18, a trip to the pub for that first legal round is essential. At 21, 'proper' Champagne feels wonderfully sophisticated and exciting. Someone hitting 30 might appreciate some fine New World wine, while 40- and 50-year-olds will probably have developed their own particular tastes for, say, Tuscan wine or top-notch single malt.

7 The **Big** Boozy Bash

It always seems like a great idea to invite the whole crowd over to party, until a couple of hours beforehand when you realise just what you're in for! Don't panic – here are all the tips you need to get it right, from picking the best wines and spirits to cocktails just made for the moment, and, of course, how to be a relaxed host.

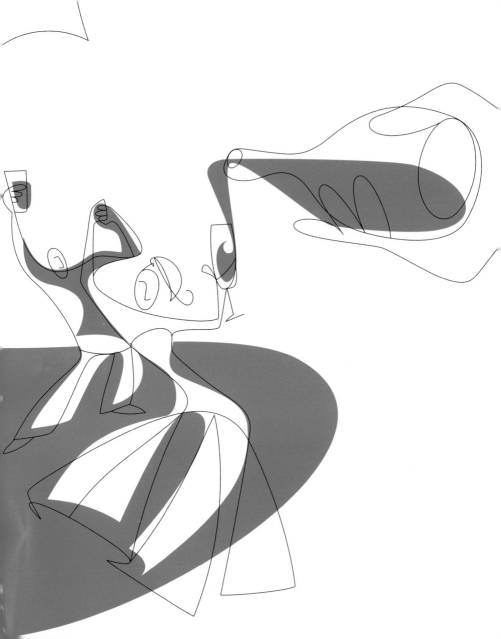

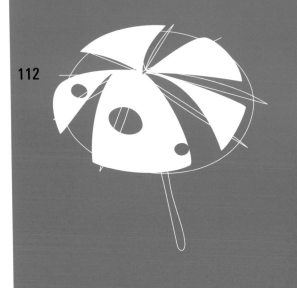

It should be the most fun, hedonistic sort of party, even for the host, but somehow, funnily, it feels stressful, having dozens of people going wild at your place! How do you provide enough decent booze to fuel a crowd and then keep it coming, chilled and fresh, all evening? How do you enjoy yourself for a moment, if you are endlessly opening bottles, pouring drinks and shaking cocktails? How come you're simply tearing your hair out, when you really should be letting it down?

Fret not. There are plenty of tips in this chapter on how to create a great, wild party for everyone, and that includes you. It's crucial to get well organised before the crowd turns up, so read on and discover why some styles of wine work much better than others, which spirits are essential at big thrashes, and which bits of kit it is necessary to leave out so your guests can help themselves.

Ah, yes, helping themselves. The true key to the big bash is to let everyone get on with it. Get the drinks right before the doorbell goes and you can forget about everything except partying like mad yourself!

THE LOWDOWN

THE Kit

The Golden Rule: when you've got a crowd heading over to your place for a few drinks, **keep it simple**. A wild, booze-fuelled party (let's be honest, that's what we are talking about here) is *not* the time to be fiddling with fancy twists of guava peel as a garnish or trying to create the most complex new flaming punch in town.

So, ensure you have all the essentials at your fingertips. The basic kit you'll need is:

— Two or more **corkscrews** (you are bound to lose at least one during the party, so borrow a couple of extras and keep them handy).

— **Ice**, ice and more ice (see page 58 for tips on how to keep things cool).

—**Citrus fruits** for long drinks and cocktails, plus a **chopping board** and **knife**. Get in a whole load of **lemons** and **limes** and you're away. Bung slices in drinks, stick wedges into cocktails, and rub pieces around the rim of glasses to make them zesty. Easy.

—**Glasses** are best hired from the same place you buy your booze. If you are offered a choice of shapes or sizes, pick **all-purpose, plain white wine glasses**, preferably with longish stems (easier to hold).

—Round up **ashtrays**, **matches**, **paper towels** and **cloths** for mopping up spilt drink, too. Be well prepared and you will enjoy your party much more!

116   A discounted case of rough old red, a few bottles of that white you enjoyed on holiday… this is the moment to get rid of them, because at the big boozy bash no one will notice, right?

Wrong. You might fool some people, but there's bound to be a know-all in the kitchen who spots your mega-discount vino in its plastic litre bottle and clocks how stingy you are. Besides, you want the wine to taste good and preferably, not to kill your best mates, don't you?

Luckily, there are clever ways to find proper bargains for big parties. First of all, in the weeks (not days) before your party, seek out **knock-down deals** in supermarkets and wine warehouses or ask about forthcoming promotions. 'Buy One, Get One Free' (BOGOF) offers are always worth looking out for.

Pick a **well-known brand** from Australia or California, if you must. I admit these are often on offer and they are reliable, if pretty boring. But there are plenty of more **interesting cheap wines** out there, particularly from Argentina, Chile, South Africa, France, Spain, Southern Italy and Portugal. These are sometimes on offer, so snap 'em up when you see 'em! These wines should keep well for a few weeks if you store the bottles lying on their sides somewhere fairly cool and dark.

Party Plonk

Big-party wines should be crowd-pleasers: **easy-going, well-balanced and fruity**. Top styles: **South African Chenin Blanc** (appley, soft, fruity); **French Sauvignon de Touraine** (drier, zesty, light); **Argentinian Malbec** (juicy, cherryish); inexpensive **Spanish reds** (ripe, versatile) and **Languedoc's vin de pays d'Oc reds** (smooth, rounded, satisfying); **Cava** (Spain's great-value bubbly).

Try before buying, if at all possible. Get a bottle to taste at home or find a store that offers open wines for sampling. Buy sale or return so you get a refund on unopened bottles.

At the big boozy bash, many will slake their thirst on **lager** – it is, after all, **cold, fresh and easy to swig down**, reaching the parts other drinks don't when you're dancing the night away. It's a shame, though, that at most parties you find the same big brand lagers, usually American, usually in cans, and usually tasting very bland.

Make your party different!

—Stock up on **lager**, but make it the bottled stuff (posher) and pick one with bags more character, such as good-quality **German** or **Czech pilsner** or **Dutch lager**. Or try **Australian sparkling ale** or good **English bitter**.

—**Little bottles** are a good idea as you are repeatedly opening a fresh, cool beer rather than hanging on to a stale, warm one.

—Or get a keg of fine **English ale** (from a local brewery or decent pub) and stick it in the kitchen for guests to pour their own.

—Or get in the **cider**. Again, avoid the mass-marketed stuff, and go for **premium bottled cider** from **England** (the West country, Herefordshire or Worcestershire) or **France** (Normandy region). Or get a **flagon** or three from a nearby **farmhouse cider** producer. Watch out for scarily high alcohol levels on 'real' ciders!

Beers
& CIDERS

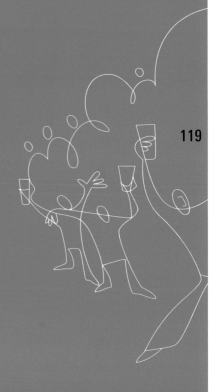

119

THE BIG BOOZY BASH

long drinks and soft drinks

Long drinks are brilliant at big parties because you can leave your guests to make them up themselves: provide the gin, vodka or scotch and a fridge full of mixers and let them get on with it. Long drinks are simple, or at least they should be on this occasion – don't bother with complex garnishes or fancy glasses, although some fun straws might be nice, if kitsch! Long drinks should also keep people happy for quite a while before they need the next one.

So what should you put out as your 'bar'? **Gin** and plain **vodka** along with **tonic** are must-haves, as is a bottle of **scotch** (see page 72) and perhaps some **tequila** – preferably gold. For mixers, make sure you stock up on loads of **tonic** (the most popular choice by far), **lemonade**, **soda** and **cola**. Consider having some diet versions of all of these.

Leave out some fresh **lemons** and **limes** (try to find organic, unwaxed ones), a little **sharp knife** and a **cutting board** for people to slice their own, and don't forget to make sure there's lots of **ice** in the freezer. Make a long drink for each guest who wants one when they arrive, but then tell them to **help themselves** after that.

Soft drinks are already there in the form of the lemonades, colas and sodas provided, but supplement these with some other ideas such as putting out a little bottle of **bitters** (splash into tonic for a touch of flavour and style), some good grown-up **cordial** (I love lemongrass and ginger) and perhaps a **tasty juice** such as cranberry. Again, keep it simple – neither host nor guests want to faff around too much at the big boozy bash!

You could go for **tequila shots**, they certainly get a party going. They are good fun and are something that works with more than a few people – just don't do it at home on your own, saddo! It goes like this: lick a little **salt** off the back of your hand, grab a quick shot of **tequila**, then quickly suck on a wedge of **lemon** or **lime**. As mouthwatering as it sounds. Or try **slammers** – **tequila** in a shot glass, topped up with a little **soda water** or **sparkling wine**, hand over the top, bang on the table and quickly splashed into the mouth while the fizz is frothing. Fab!

But let's face it, **cocktails** are classier. The best for wild parties, without question, are the groovy, easy-to-make, rum-based South American ones. The CAIPIRINHA is made simply with **lime quarters**, muddled hard with a teaspoon of **sugar syrup** before adding **ice** and **cachaça** (Brazilian sugar cane rum) or **white rum**. Add **soda** for a long version. Or try a MOJITO. Muddle **mint leaves** with a few drops of **sugar syrup**, add the juice of half a **lime** and throw the squeezed half in. Add **ice** and **soda water**, stir and add 50ml **white** or **gold rum**. Garnish with **fresh mint**.

To create the right cocktail party atmosphere, get everyone muddling or pouring (use special pourers in the necks of bottles and pour from a height), chopping mint and citrus fruit and, finally, downing the intoxicating end results!

cocktails, shots and slammers

THE PERFECT HOST

🔍 I FANCY HOSTING A 'BRING-A-BOTTLE' PARTY, BUT WILL IT BE A PROBLEM IF WE END UP WITH LOADS OF DIFFERENT DRINKS?

🅰 If you want your guests to bring a bottle, pick a theme and get your friends to stick to it. For example, plan your party around vodka (long drinks made from vodka/vodka cocktails) and ask all your mates to bring plain vodka. Or ask for sparkling wine and drink it straight or as fizzy cocktails. Provide the mixers, garnishes, etc yourself.

🔍 PLEASE TELL ME HOW TO ENJOY MYSELF WITHOUT HAVING TO OPEN BOTTLES ENDLESSLY!

🅰 Here's how – pick wines with screw caps *and* leave out several corkscrews, choose an allocated spot as the 'bar' and place everything there or in the fridge. Say firmly to each guest, as they arrive, that they must help themselves to drinks and open new bottles if they like. Then don't stand around the bar, go away and enjoy yourself!

Q WHAT IF WE RUN OUT OF BOOZE? LAST TIME I HAD A PARTY I HAD TO MAKE A DASH FOR THE BOTTLE SHOP TO RESTOCK!

A You can never have too much at a wild party. Buy sale or return and get in loads, in the knowledge you can always return unopened bottles. Never understock this kind of party – it is death to run out of grog!

Q HOW DO I REMOVE RED WINE STAINS FROM THE CARPET?

A The golden rule is to deal with any spillage immediately. Mop up as much as possible by pressing a tea towel or loads of paper towels hard into the spill. Once the towels are coming up completely dry, pour a small amount of dry white wine over the mess and mop up again. In the morning, wash thoroughly with carpet cleaner. Alternative quick fix: cover with fine table salt to soak up the spill and deal with it in the morning.

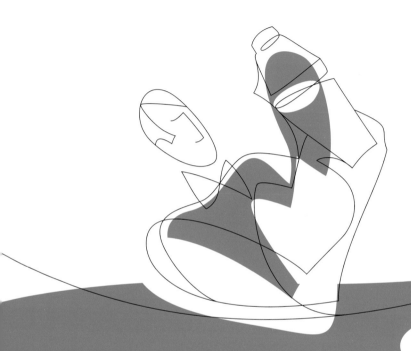

It's when you are drinking out on the town that you are most likely to be ripped off. For example, wine in restaurants can have crazily high mark-ups – just compare the prices with those of your local bottle shop. The solution is to keep your wits about you (despite the alcohol), order cannily and use the waiter or bar staff to your best advantage. Here's how…

8 out on the town

THE LOWDOWN

Why are so many of us still intimidated by ordering drinks when we are out in restaurants, clubs and bars? What is it that reduces otherwise confident people to quivering wrecks as soon as they are handed a wine list in a posh restaurant? Perhaps it's because some of the old mystery and snobbishness that used to be attached to wine still lingers in restaurants.

Choosing what to drink at home isn't scary, though, and nor should it be when you are out. If you lose your cool in a restaurant and order something you don't really want, you stand to get ripped off good and proper. Here's the lowdown on how to get the best out of restaurant wines and other drinks when out on the town – and much of that involves getting a good waiter or bar tender on your side.

The aim is to choose something good value, which suits both your food and the sense of occasion. It's no good ordering the cheap and fairly ordinary house red when your beloved has just plumped for a special birthday meal of delicate scallops. Likewise, a huge knees-up with the office team is not really the moment to get all serious and wine-buffy over the fine clarets…

Of course, being out on the town isn't just about wine. Here's more about ordering at the bar, and a 'Q&A' section devoted to some of the etiquette and plain good sense around drinking outside the home. Read on…

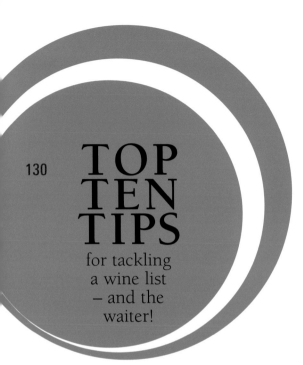

TOP TEN TIPS

for tackling a wine list – and the waiter!

1 Apart from choosing an aperitif, **pick your food first** and *then* find the wine to go with it. (Unless you are buying a very expensive and special bottle of wine, in which case do it the other way round.) Never think of them separately – make sure the **food and wine work together**.

2 Decide on exactly the **style of wine** you want – not just white or red, but dry unoaked white (Sauvignon Blanc, Riesling) or light, fruity red (Beaujolais, some Pinot Noir) – and zoom in on those bottles, rather than looking for brands, price points or countries of origin. Some wine lists are helpfully

arranged by style rather than price or country; others include useful **tasting notes**. Alternatively, **quiz the wine waiter**.

3 Check out whether there is a **wine short list** somewhere within the main tome – perhaps a selection of eight or ten wines at the beginning or the end that are **most versatile** with food. This is often a good sign in a wine list and can provide **easy pointers** if you are in a rush to order.

4 **Forget about price** until you have taken a closer look; it's no good setting yourself a **maximum budget** of £20.00 per bottle and then spotting the perfect Chablis at £22.95. See what they've got before limiting yourself.

5 **Avoid house wines** unless you know the specific bottle. House wine can be good, occasionally, but more often it is pure plonk, fobbed off on the most wine-ignorant punter. **Trade up** a notch or ask to try it before committing to a bottle, as the house wine is always open somewhere.

6 Don't ignore the **wines by the glass** (see pages 134–5). Likewise, buying in **half-bottles** can also be a canny way forward. At the other end of the spectrum, consider impressive **magnums** or even bigger for larger groups.

7 Keep an eye on the **mark-up**. Check out a restaurant's policy by comparing the price of a familiar bottle on their wine list to the cost in an off-licence. If it seems extremely over-priced, stick to tap water!

8 Talking of which, don't let anyone talk you into paying more for water than you want. There is nothing, repeat nothing, wrong with ordering **jugs of tap water** if that is what you decide to have. Mineral/spring waters can be ridiculously over-priced in restaurants.

9 Make the most of the **wine waiter**. He/she is there to help you, not to intimidate you. Get them to: describe the wine; help pick a bottle to go with a specific dish; find something at the right price; or suggest unusual and interesting selections. When offered, **taste the wine** and send back anything that seems corked (musty aroma and flat in flavour). You are the customer!

10 Make sure the wine is placed within arm's reach so that you can **help yourself** and your companions. Ensure it is kept cold, if it's a white, rosé, sparkling or even a light red.

food-friendly wines

It's rare to dine out and discover everyone in your party is ordering the same thing. More likely a group of six will plump for three steaks, one salmon, one chicken and one vegetarian pasta. So what on earth do you choose from the wine list? **Wine by the glass**, of course, is one solution (see pages 136–7), but if you want bottles, pick both white and red from the following list of **versatile wines**. These styles are especially renowned for their easy-going ability to partner many types of food, and they clash with very little.

• **Lightly oaked or unoaked Chardonnay** – fruity, fresh, but not too rich. Great with many fish and chicken dishes, mildly spiced food and creamy pasta sauces

• **Southern French Viognier** – another fruity, lively wine with plenty of character but not overwhelmed by oak. Peachy and especially tasty served up with mild curries and creamy savoury dishes, chicken and pork

• **Australian Riesling** – the riper, more robust version of European Riesling is a wow with almost any fish and seafood dish

• **Alsace whites** – wines from this part of France are famous for their food-friendly quality, especially the appley, well-balanced Pinot Blancs. Plus, when you order Alsace, it shows you know your wines

• **Tuscan reds** – Chianti Classico and co. are usually ripe, medium-bodied and have a fresh tanginess that makes them fine partners for just about all meat, including chicken. Classy choice

• **Pinot Noir** – this grape makes smooth, soft, juicy red wines the world over, from Burgundy to Chile and California, which are wonderfully food-friendly. Can be pricey, though, and quality does vary

• **Rioja Reserva** – a good mellow choice from Spain for a range of rich red meat dishes, especially lamb and beef

BUYING WINES BY THE GLASS

Gone are the days when all restaurants could muster up by the glass was a warm house white (vin de table blanc), or even warmer house red (Spanish plonk). Now any establishment worth its salt has a wide choice of **wines by the glass** – if it hasn't, it's a sign that the place doesn't take wine seriously.

Ideally, the wines by the glass will be an interesting selection so that you are encouraged to try something different without investing in a whole bottle. Do so, and you may end up ordering the full 75cl – it's a great way to **discover new wines**. Preferably, the list of by-the-glass options will be changed regularly, so that frequent diners will always find something new.

To some extent, wines should be tailored to **suit a seasonal menu**. Look out for delicate, fragrant whites in the summer and richer styles and more powerful reds in the winter. Don't ignore the sparkling wines and champagnes by the glass – many people want a flute of **fizz before dining**, but no more. Likewise, this is the moment for one glass of dry, pale fino sherry or an aperitif of very dry white that may not suit your food later on.

Take a long hard look at the wines by the glass **once the main meal is over**. Here you might find some hidden gems – ports, sherries and Madeiras by the glass, wonderful dessert wines, liqueurs, or shots of ancient and venerable spirits. Whatever you discover, never be afraid to ask the waiter if you need more help in pinning down the best choice.

ordering at the BAR

Of course, drinking on the town is not all about wining and dining. For those liquid lunches or boozy nights out, it pays to play it safe. Here's how…

—**Always order** at a bar in smaller quantities than you might think. This way your drink stays fresh and cool — half a beer or a small cocktail should taste good right to the very end — and you might drink a little less furiously this way, which is wise. Avoid the very large 250ml-plus wine glasses in particular — 250ml equates to one-third of a bottle of wine, which will turn warm after just ten minutes. Super-size me? No thanks!

—**Beware cut-price drinks**. You may be fobbed off with something sub-standard, so only go for a bargain that is tried and trusted and which you know you like.

—**Never mix** the grape and grain. Decide whether you are going to drink beer, spirits (including cocktails) or wine and stick to it. What's more, stay with the exact same spirits, beers and styles of wine if it is going to be a heavy night.

—**Hold your drink** when in a busy bar or club. You never know who might be around and unattended drinks can be spiked with drugs.

—**Think smart** (as in sophisticated and upmarket). We all love to go out drinking now and again. Raise your game and order slightly more expensive, higher-quality drinks than usual, then enjoy them slowly and savour them and you will be in for a good time. Avoid gruesome bingeing on bargain booze.

—**Quaff lots of water**, avoid smoky places and fit in some food during the evening. That way you'll enjoy drinking more and will feel better for it the next day!

THE PERFECT HOST
TIPS

Q I'M FED UP OF MEN ORDERING WINE FOR ME IN RESTAURANTS – I'D LIKE TO CHOOSE MY OWN DRINKS. HOW CAN I?

A Easy – find out a bit more about wine (from this book, and others) and drop a few wise facts when the men start taking over. They'll soon worry you might show them up, and hand the list over.

Q I OFTEN FIND WINE HORRIBLY OVER-PRICED IN RESTAURANTS – IT CAN REALLY SPOIL AN EVENING FOR ME. HOW DO I FIND BETTER VALUE?

A You need a BYO – Bring Your Own. These restaurants let you bring your own booze, and usually charge a small corkage fee for opening it. BYOs are a bit thin on the ground outside Australia, where they are very popular, but look out for them particularly in cities with lots of ethnic restaurants – for example, Muslim-owned restaurants are sometimes BYO, for obvious reasons.

🍷 I WANT TO BRING A SPECIAL BOTTLE TO OPEN IN MY FAVOURITE RESTAURANT FOR MY 40TH BIRTHDAY BUT IT IS NOT A BYO PLACE – CAN I STILL TAKE IT ALONG?

🅐 Call the restaurant first. They may well allow you to bring one special bottle, but be prepared to pay a hefty corkage fee if it goes against the norm there. And don't take something they have on their own list – it wouldn't be tactful!

🍷 MY FRIENDS ALWAYS ORDER HUGE JUGS OF POWERFUL SWEET COCKTAILS, WHICH I DISLIKE. I'D LOVE A GLASS OF SUBTLE, DRY WHITE – WHAT CAN I DO?

🅐 Develop an allergy to the cocktails – or, rather make one up! Or be the nominated driver and cry off. Or find new friends with better taste… Listen, there's one hard and fast rule in sociable drinking (and this applies to drinking games too): no one ever drinks something they don't want to. Get tough!

9

the morning after

The next day has dawned…
and it doesn't feel good. What can you do when
your house party hasn't quite finished and you're left with loads of hungover
mates in need of sustenance? It's clear, more drinks are called for! But not any
old drinks – these need to comfort and soothe, revive and reinvigorate.
Here are some suggestions to keep a cranky crowd happy.

THE LOWDOWN

It's the day after a big house party and your friends have crashed out at your place. You did a great job the night before providing brilliant cocktails, fabulous wines and astonishing after-dinner drinks. Too good a job, in fact, because now you've got to get up and start curing a whole load of hangovers!

There are two routes to take. Either you can get juicing, making all sorts of healthy non-alcoholic concoctions, or you can gently introduce more alcohol to get the party gradually going again. Both are tackled here – the healthy options are followed by tips on light alcoholic drinks for when the show really must go on!

Remember, none of these drinks is a substitute for lots of water. You will all need to rehydrate, so serve lots of cold, still mineral water alongside all the suggested drinks that follow. Add some wholesome food, some fresh air, and perhaps the odd trip to the medicine cabinet, and all should be fine. Really.

THEKit

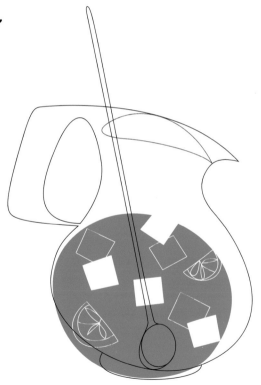

Make life easy on yourself. It's bad enough **feeling jaded** on your own, without having to entertain, feed and water a bunch of equally jaded friends. The last thing you want to make are complicated drinks that involve difficult, myriad ingredients.

To make things as simple as possible, get all the **kitchen kit** out – the juicer, the blender, the grater, the peeler – but only use sharp knives if your hands are steady enough! Sort it all out and wash it up **the night before**, if you can, so you're not hunting in dark cupboards for bits and pieces with a steaming headache at 10am the next day. **Forget the posh glasses** (they are probably dirty from the night before, anyway). It's fine – and fun – to serve hangover cures in tea mugs, tumblers, toothbrush mugs, plastic cups, **whatever comes to hand**. Serve in big batches – huge jugfuls of hangover-cure look generous, bountiful and appealing.

Don't go mad trying to make garnishes; no one is going to be impressed or, indeed, notice. They should be grateful enough that you are making *any* drinks for them! Just make sure the **essential ingredients** are to hand – a couple of days before your party, **stock up** on tabasco sauce, fresh celery, tomato juice, fresh fruit, yoghurt, ginger, honey, eggs, whatever you plan to use. That way you won't be trailing round the supermarket while your friends sleep on! Don't forget mineral water, strong tea, good coffee and paracetamol while you are at it.

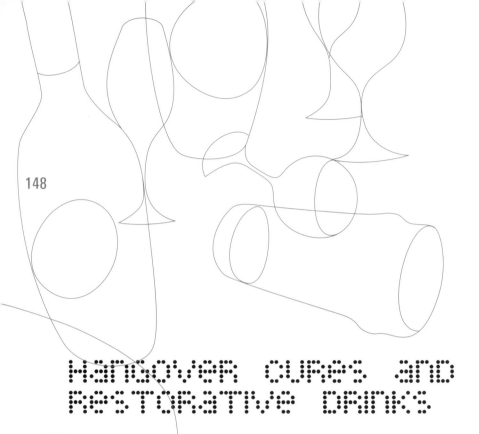

Hangover cures and restorative drinks

Start by making fun, original drinks of a non-alcoholic nature – soothing, healthy, delicious draughts that will coax your guests into feeling alive again. A couple of the reviving drinks suggested here, followed by a light meal and a brisk walk and you'll have provided the best end to a weekend party for everyone – even for those who have to drive home.

- **Citrus fruit** – but go gentle on very acidic fruit juices. A large glass of chilly, tart grapefruit juice on a dodgy stomach could be nasty! Instead, try **soothing juices** – perhaps a **gentle**, **cloudy**, **sweetish apple juice** or **pulpy**, **soft mango juice** or **squashy**, **luscious peach juice**…

- **Red berries** are nice and they're healthy, of course – try **cranberries**, **blueberries**, **strawberries** and **raspberries**. Juice or blend fresh berries, or cook and puree, and add honey and dilute to taste.

- **Bananas** have the right sweetness, they're not acidic and they fill you up as well. Use bananas to make **nutritious breakfast drinks** that are liquid meals in themselves. A great one for blending with yoghurt to make smoothies. Add honey, vanilla essence… anything you fancy (or perhaps that should be 'anything you can bear').

- **Mix the veg** – try **celery juice**, **carrot juice** and so on. Remarkably **soothing**, **healthy** and **restorative**, but not perhaps the tastiest, so mix with fruit juices. **Apple** and **carrot**, perhaps with a little fresh **ginger**, is tried and tested and works wonders.

- **Tomato juice** – try a **Virgin Mary**. Follow the recipe for **Dave's Bloody Mary** on page 153, but leave out the vodka and sherry!

• **Honey and fresh ginger** – already touched on, but they deserve their own mention. Both are unusually **comforting** and stave off nausea and tummy upsets. Make a hot drink with **milk**, **honey** and **ginger**, or **lemon**, **honey** and **ginger**, or simply add fresh ginger slices (not grated as that can taste too strong and raw) to hot water, stir in a dollop of honey and perhaps add a clove or stir with a cinnamon stick. Ahh, that's better…

• **Dairy products** – **milk**, **cream** (not too heavy), **yoghurt** (especially good) and even soft, premium **ice cream** (floating on a drink) are all **soothing** for a mild hangover. Warm milk with a little demerara sugar and plenty of nutmeg freshly grated on top is especially soporific and stomach calming after a heavy night.

• **Eggs** – the base of many a hangover cure. Frankly, raw egg is the last thing I even want to think about when hungover, but it works for millions! Each to their own, so, if you must, a classic PRAIRIE OYSTER is 2 shots of **brandy**, 1 **egg yolk**, 1 teaspoon **wine vinegar**, a dash each of **Tabasco** and **Worcestershire sauce**, and a pinch of **cayenne pepper**. Good luck.

• **Cola** – it's not clever, and it's not classy, but **lightly chilled**, **non-diet cola**, sipped slowly, works – think caffeine, sugar and fresh fizz in your mouth. Serve a big jugful with lemon slices and ice.

THE MORNING AFTER

easy alcoholic drinks

The other option, of course, is to try the **hair of the dog**. The dog that bit you, that is. This ancient expression sums up the difficulty most of us have with this proposition. The dog that bit us the night before is not a dog we actively want to go anywhere near for the time being. It's definitely not a good idea if you are severely hungover to take alcohol again – give your liver, head and dignity a chance to restore themselves. But a light hangover can be cured effectively by returning to drink, as long as you **approach it with caution**.

In other words, avoid strong liquor and try subtle, naturally low-alcohol drinks. **Sparkling wine** is usually a good one for the mildly hungover – how many wedding reception Champagnes have revived faintly jaded grooms who hit the pub the night before? At around 12%, **Champagne** is not particularly high in alcohol, it tastes **clean**, **fresh** and **appealing** to the tired palate and the bubbles deliver a zesty crisp feel as well as making sure the **alcohol kicks in** quickly. Try adding a bruised (bashed with a spoon) slice of fresh ginger to a flute for an even more vibrant, peppery kick. Or make **Buck's Fizz**, blending good quality **fresh orange juice** with perhaps a **dry cava**. Otherwise, try a fragrant, appley, chilled glass of fine **German Riesling** which often has an alcohol content of just 7–10%. Floral aromas and **crisp**, **clean fruit flavours** ease you gently into drinking again.

Away from wine, it has to be a **Bloody Mary**. I planned to put a more unusual hangover-cure cocktail in at this point, but having taken a straw poll of friends and colleagues, it became abundantly clear that the Bloody Mary is **tried and trusted** like no other. The combo of tomato juice, vodka, spices and ice is the hands-down winner. So you can take your Prairie Oysters, Corpse Revivers, Gin Fizzes, Harvey Wallbangers and Long Island Iced Teas (other less popular candidates). Here's the **all-time favourite hangover cocktail**. And this is the best recipe I've found, from the spirits writer Dave Broom:

DAVE'S BLOODY MARY Pour a large shot of **vodka**, preferably pepper flavoured (Absolut Peppar or Pieprzówka), into each glass filled with lots of **ice**. Combine **tomato juice**, **Worcestershire sauce**, **Tabasco sauce**, **white pepper**, **salt**, **celery salt**, **lime juice** and a splash of **chilled dry sherry** in a jug, measured to taste, but heavy on the tomato juice and easy on the other ingredients! Pour this mix over the vodka and ice, then stir (try using a celery stick). Start to feel better. PS: Make the night before and store in the fridge.

THE PERFECT HOST
TIPS

I DON'T WANT MY FRIENDS TO HANG AROUND ALL DAY. IF I MAKE SOME OF THESE FAB DRINKS, THEY MIGHT NEVER LEAVE!

Tell them you are making a wonderful hangover cure (non-alcoholic) as their 'one for the road'. Mix it up and serve it with a final flourish in a way that makes it clear you expect everyone to go home afterwards. Or tell them it tastes better if they have their coats on.

I CAN'T BE BOTHERED TO COOK A FULL ENGLISH BREAKFAST *AND* MAKE PERFECT BANANA SMOOTHIES.

The great thing about a drink like a smoothie is that it *is* a breakfast on its own. A bit of toast is all that might be called for when you're drinking something this filling and good, so you can put the frying pan back in the cupboard.

🍷 I BOUGHT GOOD CHAMPAGNE FOR BRUNCH, BUT FORGOT TO CHILL IT IN TIME. HOW CAN I GET IT COLD, QUICK?

🅰 Bung it in the freezer for a quick ice blast – after 10 minutes, transfer it to the fridge. Don't forget about it though – it won't taste good if it's too cold, and if it freezes hard it might just break!

🍷 I'VE ONLY GOT CHEAP, NASTY OJ BUT A GOOD BOTTLE OF FIZZ – WILL MY BUCK'S FIZZ TASTE OKAY?

🅰 Sorry, no. It's much better to splash out on top-notch, fresh orange juice and use a cheaper sparkling wine like cava. The orange is the dominant flavour in the drink. Best of all, squeeze your own juice…

A WORD ON PARTY SNACKS

Serious dining (and wining) is dealt with in some depth in Chapter 2, where you'll find lots of tips on how to **match wine and food**. The basic message is to **balance like with like** – make sure light dishes go with lighter wine; sweeter puddings with honeyed styles; the heartiest feast with powerful, rich vino.

But what if you are having only a few little snacks? The same rule applies – balance up the food and drink. Try crisp, sparkling wines with simple, **light fish**, **seafood** and **vegetarian canapés**; light, zesty unoaked whites like Sauvignon Blanc with salty snacks like **crisps or nuts**; fino or manzanilla sherry with **olives**; richer whites like Chardonnay with richer, **creamy chicken** or **salmon snacks**; and soft, fruity reds with savoury bites like **sausage rolls**, **cold ham**, **pâtés** or full-flavoured **cheesy nibbles**. Tannic, robust reds are not a good choice at a party where light snacks are being served – their flavours are just too strong.

When planning snacks or even a simple buffet, do watch out for some ingredients that can severely affect the wines/cocktails/other delicious drinks on offer! Cut back on chilli peppers, for example, if you want the wine to taste good, as a very hot element in the food **kills the flavour** of the wine. Vinegar is another wine destroyer, so go easy on the salad dressing. Mustard, pickles, gherkins and capers have the same effect; and don't even try to show off a posh Champagne if you have anchovies/cockles/anything else in brine on the table (try stronger, dry fino sherry instead).

Leave the sharp dressing, piquant mustard and so on in a separate bowl for guests to help themselves, but don't swamp all the food with such wine-unfriendly condiments. Stick to **fresh**, **simple**, **undressed food** if you want the drinks to shine through! If you do want very **spicy snacks**, it would be best to stick with lager or other beer or soft drinks.

A WORD ON PARTY SNACKS

BEST BRANDS

Don't buy dirt-cheap, poor-quality spirits, even for mixing and cocktails. Taste the difference when you pick the right labels. Here are some ideas:

Gin – Pick those with over 40% alcohol; they have more character.
• **Best** – Tanqueray, Bombay Sapphire, Plymouth Gin, Larios, Hendricks

Vodka – Most of the top vodkas come from Eastern Europe and Scandinavia.
• **Best** – Absolut, Finlandia, Wyborowa, Grey Goose

Brandy – Look for the quality category, not brand names, for Cognac. Buy basic 'VS'-level for mixing cocktails or long drinks; go for 'VSOP' or higher for sipping.

Whisky – Very subjective, but try Bell's 8-year-old, or the Irish Jameson. Do pick the smokey single malts from the Scottish islands for sipping (Talisker, Laphroaig). For Bourbon, try Maker's Mark or Bulleit.

Tequila – Try gold tequila as well as white.
• **Best** – José Cuervo, Porfidio, Tres Magueyes, Real Hacienda, El Tesoro

Rum – Go for gold or white rum for cocktails; dark rum for sipping.
• **Best** – Havana Club, Mount Gay, Cockspur, El Dorado, Appleton Estate

INDEX

ale 33, 88, 118
Amaretto 41
aperitifs 29, 31, 32-3
Armagnac 41, 67, 73
Asti 36, 105
banana drinks 149
bar drinks 138-9
beers 33, 38, 39, 57, 88, 90, 118
Bellini 99
Benedictine 41, 67, 77
bitters 15, 121
Black Velvet 67
Bloody Mary 153
Bourbon 41, 55, 67, 89
brandy 41, 73, 158; Brandy
  Alexander 66
Buck's Fizz 152, 155
buying drink 108, 117, 125
Caipirinha 122
Calvados 41, 67, 73
Campari 53, 56
cava 32, 51, 97, 117, 152, 155
Champagne 32, 96-7, 107,
  109,155; Champagne Cocktail
  16, 99

Chartreuse 41, 67, 77, 78
chocolate 64
cider 38, 89, 70, 118; Cider Cup
  69
citrus fruit 115, 121, 149
Clairette de Die 105
coffee: iced 57; Irish 77; liqueur
  64
Cognac 41, 77
Cointreau 17, 21, 41, 67
cola 39, 150
cooling drinks 49, 58
cordials 38, 39, 57, 100, 107, 121
'corkage' 108, 140, 141
Cosmopolitan 17
cranberry juice 17, 33, 70,
  85,121
crèmant 97
Daiquiris 18, 24; Frozen
  Strawberry 18, 55
elderflower: cordial 39, 100,
  107; pressé 33; Elderfower
  Syrup 56; Ginger and
  Elderflower Cordial 57
fruit 49; garnishes 25, 49, 64;
  ice cubes 49; see also citrus
  fruit; Daiquiris

garnishes 15, 25, 49, 64
gin 33, 120–21, 158; Gin Fizz 19
Ginger and Elderflower Cordial
  57
glasses 14, 30-31, 58, 59, 64;
  hiring 115
Grand Marnier 41, 67, 77
Guinness: Black Velvet 67
hangovers 90, 145, 147-53
Horse's Neck 67
ice cubes 14, 25, 115; fruit 49
infusions 64, 65
Irish coffee 77
Irish whiskey 71, 72
juices 39, 56, 70, 79, 121,
  145, 147-9
Kir/Kir royales 52, 99
lager 38, 89, 118
lemonade, homemade 39, 56
limeade, homemade 56
liqueurs 41, 67, 77, 78, 86
Madeira 33, 41, 77
Manhattan 20
Margarita 21, 24, 55
Marmalade and Ginger Tea 71
Martini 22, 24, 33
mead 70, 100

Mint Julep 55
Mojito 122
mulled wine 64, 69, 70, 100
non-alcoholic/soft drinks 33,
  38, 39, 47, 56-7, 70, 79, 90-1,
  100, 145, 149
Pacharan 77
Peach Shake 53
Pimm's 56
Piña Colada 85
port 41, 76, 89; white 33, 56
porter 88
potcheen 71
Prairie Oyster 150
pressés 33, 100
Prosecco 97
punch, non-alcoholic 70
restaurants 140-1; wines
  126, 129, 130-7
rum 18, 65, 67, 73, 122, 158

sake 39
Sangria 52
Sea Breeze 85
sherry 33, 41, 86
slammers 122
sloe gin 56
smoothies 149, 154
snacks, party 156-7
soft drinks see non-alcoholic
  drinks
spices 64
spritzers 52
stout 88
sugar syrup 25
tea: iced 57; Marmalade and
  Ginger 71
tequila 21, 121, 122, 158;
  Tequila Sunrise 23
toasts 94-5, 100, 106-7, 109
tomato juice 149

vermouths 20, 22, 53, 56
Virgin Mary 149
vodka 17, 56, 65, 67, 85,
  124, 158
wassail cup 70
water 39, 132, 145
wedding cups 100
whisk(e)y 20, 72, 121, 158; Irish
  71, 72; single malt 41, 72, 78,
  89; see also Bourbon
wine 116-17; dessert/pudding
  33, 36, 43, 77, 105; mulled
  64,69, 70, 100; red 35, 36, 38,
  50-1, 52, 74, 75, 78-9, 103;
  sparkling 32, 43, 51, 75, 79,
  97, 105, 107, 152; spiced 100;
  white 32, 35, 36, 38, 50, 74,
  75, 79, 86, 91, 103; see also
  restaurants
Woo Woo 85

Acknowledgements

Thanks to the great team at Quadrille; to Rachel Williams of Kino cocktail bar in Exeter;
and to wine and spirit experts Dave Broom and Chris Orr. Books: *The Craft of the Cocktail* by
Dale DeGroof (Proof Publishing) is an invaluable and comprehensive guide, while *The Boys'
Beer Book* by Jonny Goodall (Mitchell Beazley) is a fun beginner's guide to the subject.